CW00348443

what we mean when we
talk about leadership

what we mean
when we talk about

leadership

Stuart Crainer and Des Dearlove

infiniteideas

Copyright ©Suntop Media Limited, 2015

The right of Stuart Crainer and Des Dearlove to be identified as the authors of this book has been asserted in accordance with the Copyright, Designs and Patents Act 1988.

First published in 2015 by
Infinite Ideas Limited
www.infideas.com

All rights reserved. Except for the quotation of small passages for the purposes of criticism or review, no part of this publication may be reproduced, stored in a retrieval system or transmitted in any form or by any means, electronic, mechanical, photocopying, recording, scanning or otherwise, except under the terms of the Copyright, Designs and Patents Act 1988 or under the terms of a licence issued by the Copyright Licensing Agency Ltd, 90 Tottenham Court Road, London W1T 4LP, UK, without the permission in writing of the publisher. Requests to the publisher should be emailed to the Permissions Department, permissions@infideas.com.

A CIP catalogue record for this book is available from the British Library
ISBN 978–1–908984–51–7

Brand and product names are trademarks or registered trademarks of their respective owners.

Printed and bound in Great Britain by Marston Book Services Ltd, Oxfordshire

Contents

Introduction

Over the last twenty-five years we have interviewed hundreds of leaders from around the world. They have been young and old. Some were entrepreneurs just setting out on a commercial adventure. Others were experienced C-suite veterans, leaders who had lived through the ups and downs of corporate life. Still others were drawn from NGOs, charities and social enterprises. We have talked with sports people, leaders from the medical profession, executive coaches, academic thought leaders and with classrooms filled with ferociously bright and competitive MBA students all intent on becoming leaders.

Looking over the articles, notes, videos and other outputs from these scores of encounters, conversations and interviews it becomes clear that humility rather than heroism seems to lie at the heart of really effective and inspiring leadership. The best leaders are often brilliantly ordinary, while their results are defiantly extraordinary. Indeed, there is often a reverse correlation between the willingness of people to talk about leadership and the greatness of their leadership. Those who opine about their neat leadership philosophy and unique take on leadership tend, in our experience, to be personally and professionally unimpressive. It is notable that the unquestionably great leaders tend to downplay the reality of their leadership. They get on with it, give credit to their colleagues and teams, and proceed with purpose.

We hope we have captured this extraordinariness as well as the ordinariness in *What We Mean When We Talk About Leadership*. It is a smorgasbord of leadership rather than neatly compartmentalized.

1

Indeed, one of our conclusions from interviewing and encountering hundreds of leaders is that they defy overly neat categorization.

Our objective with the book is simple: to provide accessible, pithy inspiration for all those who practice and experience leadership – and, one way or another, this applies to nearly all of us.

Leadership is an act of exploration and so, too, is the study of leadership. So, if you are a leader and have a story to tell, please let us know.

Stuart Crainer and Des Dearlove
October 2015

Defining leadership #1

First things first. Mention the word leadership in a classroom or in conversation in a suitably convivial bar and people always become hard-boiled, demanding a definition of what you mean by leadership. Mention marketing or strategy or the meaning of life and they are less demanding. But, with leadership, definitions are required.

This thirst for defining leadership as a term is, in itself, interesting. Leadership perplexes us. Its ambiguity worries us. And yet, we know it when we experience it; good leadership (and bad leadership) are palpable. We know leadership when it has an impact on us. We feel that it should be black and white, easily defined and understood. That it isn't and cannot be is the first frustration of leadership. There are many others.

Writing this book, we found ourselves in a conference call with three leadership academics at one of the world's leading business schools. They were just about to set up a new leadership center which was well endowed with funding from a successful business leader. They talked for a while. And then they talked some more. Eventually, we asked if there was a working definition of leadership which they used. What did they mean when they talked about leadership? Silence. More silence. 'Not exactly,' said the director of the new center with an entertaining degree of awkwardness.

So, though we thirst for a neat and tidy definition of what leadership is, such definitions are thin on the ground. Little wonder perhaps that researchers at the UK's Reading University are examining the brains of business, military and other leaders to better understand what makes them effective leaders.

When we spoke with Gianpiero Petriglieri of the French business school INSEAD, one of the most original thinkers on the subject these days, we inevitably got around to his definition of leadership. 'I take issue with this idea of leadership as the ability to get others to do things that they wouldn't otherwise have done. That's a traditional definition,' he bridled.

> And I think we'd be a lot better off with a definition of leadership as having the courage, commitment, ability and the trust to articulate, embody and help realize the story of possibility – for a group of people, at a point in time. That is closer to what leaders really do. First you need to have the courage to do something. You need commitment. You can't just do it for a day or two. You do need some skills, but you also need to be entrusted. It is something that comes from within and is also grounded in some group at a certain point in time. If you want to be 'a leader' you are no one's leader.

Gianpiero's pointed observations ring true. When it comes to understanding leadership, we have moved from directive leadership, and leadership derived from authority and power, to a greater belief in the interactive nature of leadership and leadership by consent. 'I define leadership as leaders inducing followers to act for certain goals that represent the values and motivations – the wants and needs, the aspirations and expectations – of both leaders and followers,' wrote the leadership theorist, James McGregor Burns. Leadership is – fashionably perhaps – as inclusive as never before. We practice leadership with people rather than inflicting leadership on them.

Our definition and understanding of leadership now stretches beyond notions of hierarchy, job titles and being told to do something. Our view of leadership is more broad ranging. Leadership is not a rarity. We are willing to accept that it takes leadership to make a busy restaurant kitchen work efficiently, to enable a sports team to perform at its best or for a medical operation to be successfully carried out.

'Leadership means vision, cheerleading, enthusiasm, love, trust, verve, passion, obsession, consistency, the use of symbols, paying attention as illustrated by the content of one's calendar, out-and-out drama (and the management thereof), creating heroes at all levels, coaching, effectively wandering around, and numerous other things. Leadership must be present at all levels of the organization,' argued Tom Peters and Nancy Austin in *A Passion for Excellence*.

'Every teacher in a classroom is a leader,' Dame Mary Marsh told us – and she has worked as a headteacher as well as leading major charitable organizations. 'Leadership is not just at the top, it's everywhere. I don't think we're good at acknowledging that, and recognizing where people are developing their leadership capacity – at home, in the family, in schools and colleges, in the community and all parts of organizations.'

Yet, while the net of leadership has widened, many of the institutions and systems of traditional notions of leadership continue. It is depressingly true, for example, that few women manage to reach the highest levels of organizations. Only 12.5 percent of the directors of FTSE-100 companies are women. There are a host of similarly dismal statistics available.

Look around, and there are still ornate organizational charts which map out labyrinthine corporate hierarchies. There are still job titles and uniforms which suggest someone should be a leader. It is a suggestion which many relish.

We still have a long way to go in our understanding of leadership. 'I see leadership as our version of the dark ages. In the sixteenth century whenever we didn't understand something – an earthquake or crops failing or disease – we would ascribe it to God. But then came the Enlightenment and we discovered new areas of physics and chemistry, so we could offer different explanations for earthquakes and crop failures,' lamented Jim Collins, author of *Good to Great*, when we spoke. 'In the twentieth and twenty-first century, when we're looking at the social world, the man-made world, we are still in the dark ages. This is shown by our predilection for looking for leadership answers. Leadership is to the twentieth century what God was to the sixteenth century. That doesn't mean you have to become an atheist. But if you stop looking for answers that are always either God or leadership you will find other underlying factors.'

Part of the problem is that there is a generously proportioned mythology around leadership. Control, direction and manipulation are the resonant leadership chorus. The preoccupation of many people for decades has been on identifying the characteristics of successful leaders. This, it was thought, would unlock leadership's Holy Grail. It is an impossible task. Leadership is highly individual. There was only one Steve Jobs. Emulation is pointless and charisma a smokescreen.

Leadership is much more multifaceted and fraught than was once thought. And it is much more open. There is – or should be – nothing elitist about leadership. It is open to all. Not everyone has the will to lead but, for those with the desire, leadership is there, like a jewel in the snow, ready to be picked up, cherished and eventually passed on.

Resources

The full interview with Jim Collins can be found in our book *Leadership: Organizational Success through Leadership* (McGraw Hill, 2013).

Our interview with Gianpiero Petriglieri is available at www.thinkers50.com. He is worth following on Twitter: @gpetriglieri.

What we really know about leadership

Leadership is universal and timeless. People have led and thought about leadership since the beginning of time – from Aristotle to Shakespeare, Sun Tzu to von Clausewitz, from Machiavelli to José Mourinho. And yet it was only in the 1980s that the study of leadership exploded into life. From a theoretical byway it became an intellectual-heavy industry with hardly a day passing by without a new theory, treatise or celebration of a leader.

Most of the books and thinking on leadership have a familiar feel. They celebrate the leadership of Barack Obama, Nelson Mandela, Sheryl Sandberg or some other regularly lauded leader. There are useful lessons to be drawn from such remarkable lives, but leadership is about more than great men and women. So, too, must it be more than a predictable litany of largely unattainable competencies.

The reality is that leadership is not neat and tidy, an arena filled with heroic figures to whom we might one day aspire. Leadership is often messy and complicated. '[Leaders] lead by sharing power, by spreading initiative and responsibility. They resolve tensions and conflicts that paralyze organizations from realizing larger objectives. They create and identify resources that allow the group effort to be carried out. It is very difficult to describe. Leadership is a very complex social process. Inevitably any kind of discussion like this makes it seem more orderly than it really is,' says Harvard Business School's Rakesh Khurana. 'Leaders

7

make decisions, they act on them, they realize that they are right or wrong. In some cases they revise them, in other cases they reverse them. Misunderstandings are frequent.'

Cut away the sheer messiness of leadership, the heroes and the hyperbole, not to mention the psychology, and what do we really understand about leadership in the second decade of the twenty-first century?

Leadership is not science

If management is prose, leadership is poetry. And, like the best poetry, it is resonant with meaning yet unwilling to be neatly explained or categorized. Those who profess to nail leadership down to four factors or five characteristics are liable to provide disappointment rather than enlightenment.

Leadership is about followers

Leaders are defined by their followers. The subject of followership has only recently attracted attention from researchers, but it lies at the heart of leadership. 'We haven't paid enough attention to leading as something that the leader does on behalf of others. We have looked much more at one side of the leadership relationship, which is from the leader to the follower, and we've neglected the other side, from the follower to the leader,' INSEAD's Gianpiero Petriglieri told us.

Leadership is a team game

Increasingly, leadership is practiced as part of a team. A board is a leadership team – or should be. Likewise, leaders often hunt in pairs. (In his work on *consiglieri*, Richard Hytner provides interesting insights into this new perspective on leadership.)

Leadership is universal

Ask anyone to come up with a list of the great leaders and the sad truth is that 90 percent of them will be men. This imbalance is a continuing reality in organizations worldwide. The opportunities being missed by such blinkered thinking are enormous and enormously depressing.

One significant effort to redress the balance is '10,000 Women', a Goldman Sachs philanthropic initiative implemented in collaboration with leading business schools. This is a $100 million, multi-year investment to provide underserved women with a practical business education and the support services they need to grow their businesses and create jobs for their communities. The program is delivered in twenty-two countries including India, China, Brazil, Nigeria, Turkey, Afghanistan and Rwanda. Early results show that more than 70 percent of graduates increase revenues, and 50 percent hire additional employees within six months of graduation.

Any contemporary understanding of leadership must acknowledge its inclusivity rather than regarding leadership in exclusive terms. Leadership is for all, by all.

Leadership can be learned and developed

There are natural leaders who effortlessly practice leadership. But there are many more leaders who have worked hard at developing and learning the skills they need to lead. The worldwide leadership development industry is not an exercise in pyramid selling – though it sometimes feels like that when you witness some of its most tawdry elements – but is fulfilling an important need. Leaders need to be developed.

Leadership is personal

Leadership defies generalization. Most leaders have learned along the way, borrowing and stealing ideas, tactics and tips. The result has to be authentically them. Otherwise, it won't work. People are increasingly adept at smelling out fakes and falsity. They demand authenticity from their leaders.

Leadership is important

There are furious and long-lasting debates about the nature of leadership, but there are precious few people who argue that it is not important. Indeed, the reach of leadership is expanding. It is acknowledged, for example, that leadership has a crucial role to play in education and healthcare. Teachers are leaders. Surgeons are also leaders – and so, too, are nurses.

None of these elements of leadership provide automatic or straightforward clarity. Leadership is not a single light waiting to be switched on, but a complex and sometimes inspiring network of illumination and inspiration.

Resources

Richard Hytner's book *Consiglieri* (Profile, 2014) looks at the sometimes shadowy figures behind the great leaders of our times.

Our interview with Rakesh Khurana can be found in our book *Management* (McGraw Hill, 2013).

For more information on the 10,000 Women initiative visit http://www.goldmansachs.com/citizenship/10000women/

Becoming a leader   #3

I remember how weird it felt when I first became a fire captain, after almost twelve years of being a front-line firefighter. I didn't completely understand the root of these feelings but I quickly learned that as a captain the funny sarcastic remark I would make to another firefighter as their peer was now taken in a much different way. Although I didn't feel I had changed, in the minds of my crew I was indeed different – I was their leader. When I became a battalion chief, I noticed that these feelings returned but this time at a much deeper level. As I explored these feelings, I recognized that what I was feeling was a lack of confidence, a feeling of being an actor (a firefighter dressed in a chief's cloak), a feeling of inadequacy.

So says Scott Peltin, co-author of *Sink, Float, or Swim* and chief performance officer at Tignum, who held leading positions in the US fire service for twenty-five years.

Careers develop and the leaps are often demanding, sometimes perilous. Leadership transitions – from general management to senior management and from there to leadership – are fraught with pitfalls.

There is a brilliant Dilbert cartoon in which the eponymous hero contemplates such a transition: 'Now that I'm CEO, what am I supposed to actually do?' The answer is quick: 'You're supposed to make superficial statements about how good the company is, then hope something lucky happens and profits go up. It's called leadership, sir.'

In their work, Andrew and Nada Kakabadse identify three critical transitions. The first is appointment to a general management role. 'The individual no longer holds an operational role requiring the exercise of functional skills and service delivery excellence. Organizational systems and processes need to be innovatively integrated for high-quality delivery of goods/services to the market. The learning in this transition is: respect organizational processes and cross-departmental teamwork,' they counsel.

The next transition occurs when a high performing general manager is appointed to a top team role. This is how the Kakabadses explain this leap:

> The demand is for a higher-order level of intellect in order to design value adding strategy within dynamic market conditions, while displaying sensitive stakeholder engagement skills. Emotional and political intelligence is necessary to have a spread of actors identify with the vision/strategy. From making organizational processes more efficient, the individual has to reconsider the purpose and, in turn, the design of the organization.

> The learning in this transition is from making the value proposition of the enterprise work to redefining the value proposition of the firm. The challenge is to mold a harmonious team from individuals who may have previously pursued their own agendas. This demands clear thinking and a sensitive handling of powerful egos. In effect, being independently minded, putting forward a coherent argument and yet being a team player displaying 'mountains' of wisdom, are fundamental aspects of learning to negotiate through the second transition.

The final transition is when a successful CEO or Senior Vice President is offered a position on the board. Andrew and Nada Kakabadse explain:

> The key development in Transition 3 is from taking charge and driving strategy forward to scrutinizing strategy and the sensitive facilitation of relationships. In so doing, senior management need to be facilitated to 'own' the governance challenges facing the enterprise and thus work in partnership with the board so that in-

novative governance becomes a daily discipline. The prime task is to spot the vulnerabilities facing the organization and to convince others that action needs to be taken and then monitor how that action is applied. Designing governance protocols that work and influencing from a distance are the core skills of Transition 3. So too is leaving one's ego at home.

For over twenty years, Linda Hill of Harvard Business School has studied people moving into leadership positions, particularly high potential talent moving into management for the first time. Her early research followed a small number of managers over the course of the first year in a leadership position. The results formed part of her 1992 book *Becoming a Manager*.

Over the years Hill observed the challenge of that first leadership position becoming ever more difficult. 'One of the reasons people find the transition challenging,' says Hill, 'is because of a number of misconceptions they have about the role. New leaders assume that they will have a lot of authority and power and be able to exercise that freely. In fact, they often find that they are constrained because of all the connections and relationships that they need to deal with in order to do their job as leader. The sooner that they learn to manage those networked relationships, the sooner they will get to grips with their new role.'

The people we have spoken to have frequently echoed Linda Hill's findings. Leaders often feel powerless. Sometimes they are. Organizations switch to autopilot and carry on regardless of what the leader would like to happen. We have witnessed this happening in organizations.

Leadership is not power.

Another myth is that authority naturally flows from the leadership position. Direct reports do what they are told because the leader told them to. Leaders soon discover this is not the case in reality. (This is still largely the case in Japan where saying 'no' to your boss is unheard of.) 'Instead,' says Linda Hill, 'the new leader needs to demonstrate character, the intention to do the right thing, and competence in their new role, which does not have to be technical prowess but might as easily be a willingness to ask questions and to listen. Plus they need to show they can use the influence that comes from their connections within the organization.'

Showing the team who's boss immediately after they arrive in a new position is a common mistake new leaders make. Compliance and control, exercised through formal power, will not prove effective for long. 'Better to share power and influence than order,' says Hill. Equally managing one-to-one is useful, but new leaders need to create a team atmosphere, and build a collaborative, team-driven context for individuals to operate within.

Finally, new leaders need to create the conditions for success for their team. This means sticking up for their team, and using their power and influence to further the interests of the group.

Resources

Linda A. Hill, 'Becoming the Boss', *Harvard Business Review*, (January 2007).

Andrew and Nada Kakabadse's work can be found at www.kakabadse.com.

What leaders do, really

Mid-way through the Wimbledon Men's Singles Final the television cameras scanned the crowd in the royal box. There were past winners, sporting greats, politicians and celebrities of various degrees of permanence. Among them was a single figure who appeared less intent on the irresistible rise of Novak Djokovic and more on the smart phone in his hand. He was Sir Martin Sorrell, the CEO of WPP.

For the modern leader there is no rest from the steady stream of emails, the demands on their time. There is no hiding place. Sixty percent of CEO time is taken up by meetings; CEOs spend 25 percent of their time on phone calls and at public events; only 15 percent of CEO time is spent working alone. It has been estimated in the *California Management Review* that managers can spend two to three hours each day reading, sending and responding to emails. And then there are mundane traditional tasks – more research suggests that, on average, paperwork and related tasks consume 11.6 hours per week or approximately 25 percent of a manager's time, with senior managers both spending more time on these tasks and finding it more disruptive than middle managers.

At the very top, there appears a relish for such demands. Sir Martin famously promises to reply to anyone in WPP who emails him within twenty-four hours. He calculates that for anyone to bother the CEO it has to be something important. (We have emailed Sorrell and he is true to his word.)

Talking with one CEO, he summed up his modus operandi: 'The reality is that every time I am on the move, I make a call; every time I have a break I call someone. I go through a mental list of who I haven't spoken to for a while or someone who I know has a new piece of work on, or family news – they've just had a new baby or something.'

And yet, here was a man clearly happy in his work. 'The life of a CEO is not for everyone,' he told us. 'It is a grueling, stressful and often lonely, existence. It is physically, mentally and emotionally demanding. And, of course, there is no guarantee of success or even survival in the post. So why do it? Because, on a good day, it is also the best job in the world.' (We should note that for this individual the best job in the world was his for only a couple of years before an internal spat saw him ejected.)

Most jobs come with a job description, a lengthy list of the exact parameters of responsibility. But when you reach leadership roles, the job descriptions come to an end. You are left alone to make it up as you go along. The only sure thing is that you will be expected to deliver results.

The loneliness can be oppressive – and partly explains the rise of the executive coaching industry. Not knowing what it is you should do or when or with who, offers more freedom than most executives have usually experienced in the corporate cocoon. In their previous incarnations executives have often been purveyors of certainty; as leaders they find that uncertainty rules. It can bewilder even the best prepared.

Little coherent research has been done as to how leaders do and should manage their daily working lives. ('Filling out a six-page academic survey is rarely high on a CEO's daily to-do list,' reflects London Business School's Rajesh Chandy.) Indeed, the reality largely went unexplored until Henry Mintzberg's *The Nature of Managerial Work*, was published in 1973. Instead of accepting pat answers to perennial questions, Mintzberg went in search of executive reality. He simply observed what a number of managers actually did. The resulting book blew away the managerial mystique.

Rather than spending time contemplating the long term, Mintzberg found that managers were slaves to the moment, moving from task to task with every move dogged by another diversion, another call. The median time spent on any one issue was a mere nine minutes – remember this was nearly a quarter of a century before email. In *The Nature of Managerial Work*, Mintzberg identifies the characteristics of the manager at work. The manager:

- performs a great quantity of work at an unrelenting pace;
- undertakes activities marked by variety, brevity and fragmentation;
- has a preference for issues which are current, specific and non-routine;
- prefers verbal rather than written means of communication;
- acts within a web of internal and external contacts;
- is subject to heavy constraints but can exert some control over the work.

This may sound familiar.

Over thirty years later in *Managing*, Mintzberg revisited the subject of the 1973 book. He argues that the nature of managerial work hasn't actually changed:

> The content of managing changes all the time – what you're dealing with, how your industry is structured – but the process hasn't changed. The one big thing is the Internet and especially email, but I think those forms of communications just reinforce problematic behavior. So I think they're just making it worse, but I don't think they're changing management fundamentally. One thing that I admit has changed is that management has been ignored in favor of leadership.

(The relationship between management and leadership is often discussed. We regard leadership as management on steroids, heightened and intense, but from the same essence.)

Mintzberg contends that though communication is a huge part of the job of management – managers spend 50 percent of their time, in some cases, on communication – this is nothing new. He cites a 1940s study of Swedish managing directors which found that they were inundated with reports and couldn't keep up. The world has changed, but the essence and frustrations remain largely consistent. Leadership is a 24/7 job.

Resources

www.bnet.com/blog/business-research/study-how-ceos-really-spend-their-time/1123

Henry Mintzberg was the recipient of the Lifetime Achievement Award at Thinkers50 2015. More of his sometimes trenchant, often entertaining and usually illuminating views can be found at www.henrymintzberg.com

Kings and queens of context

Inflexibility is leadership suicide. Look back to Henry Ford who stuck rigidly to his policy of mass production and limited choice for consumers. It worked – for a while. Having given the market what it wanted, Ford presumed that more of the same was also what it required. He was reputed to have kicked a slightly modified Model T to pieces, such was his commitment to the unadulterated version. When other manufacturers added extras, Ford kept it simple and dramatically lost ground. The company's reliance on the Model T nearly drove it to self-destruction. Things had moved on, the world had changed.

The most disappointing and perplexing thing about leadership is that it depends. It depends on circumstances. It depends on other people. It depends on timing. It depends on a plethora of elements over which the humble and human leader has very little control.

What it depends on most is the context. The best leaders are kings and queens of context. Either their timing is right (often repeatedly) or they are able to shape the context to fit their own leadership style.

Rather than impose themselves on the group, leaders have to find a way to lead that fits in with the group. 'Inevitably, the leader has to invent a leadership style that suits the group,' leadership guru Warren Bennis told us. 'The standard models, especially command and control, simply don't work. The heads of groups have to act decisively, but never arbitrarily. They have to make decisions without limiting the perceived autonomy of the other participants. Devising and maintaining an atmosphere in which others can put a dent in the universe is the leader's creative act.'

Different situations and contexts require different styles of leader. This is the essence of situational theory. From this comes contingency theory, in which situational variables are taken into account to select the most appropriate leadership style in a given set of circumstances.

In their work in the late 1960s Paul Hersey and Ken Blanchard identified four leadership styles that could be used in different situations: telling – an autocratic style for when subordinates appeared unable or unwilling to do what is required; selling – which is sometimes seen as a coaching-type style; participating – where there is shared decision making between the leader and followers, and the leader adopts a facilitating role; and delegating – which, once the leader has identified the task, involves handing responsibility for carrying out a task to the followers.

Meanwhile, psychologist Fred E Fiedler outlined a contingency leadership model in which effectiveness relates to two factors: leadership style and situational control – the control and influence conferred on the leader because of the situation. These depended on a number of other factors, such as the relationship between the leader and followers, whether the task is a structured task or not, and how much power the leader has within the organization.

In truth, context is – like so much of leadership – something of a grey area. Context inevitably changes. Context can be fleeting. Bull markets become bears; comfortable niches are suddenly open to all-comers; a rich inheritance can quickly be squandered. Little wonder then that some leaders are effective during one period and then not during another: Winston Churchill was an effective leader in wartime, but not in peacetime, for example. What works today, won't work tomorrow.

But shouldn't leadership be concerned with changing – or at least shaping – context? If context is the more powerful force, our entire idea of the power of leaders is turned on its head. If context is queen, how much power do leaders actually have?

'To survive in the twenty-first century we're going to need a new generation of leaders, not managers,' said Warren Bennis. 'The distinction is an important one. Leaders conquer the context – the volatile, turbulent, ambiguous surroundings that sometimes seek to conspire against us and will surely suffocate us if we let them – while managers surrender to it.'

Context is the landscape through which a leader must navigate and guide their followers. Some landscapes are more rugged than others. Some have a neat road through them; others are uncharted. A gently undulating landscape can turn mountainous and treacherous. Some leaders are better at adapting to changing context than others.

Conquering the context is a lot to ask and harks back to heroic notions of leadership. For most leaders the context is there to be shaped, adapted and influenced rather than conquered. Living with and leading within a particular context is a subtle art. The best leaders are able to fit in without seeming to do so. They are as apparently comfortable as fish in water – and it doesn't appear to matter whether the water is crystal cold lake water or the murkiest, warmest sea water.

'Great leaders are able to read the context and respond accordingly. They tap into what exists and bring more to the party. In management jargon, they add value. This involves a subtle blend of authenticity and adaptation; of individuality and conformity,' Rob Goffee, co-author of *Why Should Anyone Be Led By You?* told us.

> The thing with effective leaders is that they do not simply react to context. They also shape it by conforming enough. This is the skill element. This involves knowing when and where to conform. Without this, leaders are unlikely to survive or make the connections they need to build successful relationships with others. To be effective, the leader needs to ensure his or her behaviors mesh sufficiently with the organizational culture to create traction. Leaders who fail to mesh will simply spin their wheels in isolation from their followers.

Goffee, and his co-author Gareth Jones, talk of 'authentic chameleons', leaders who are able to be true to themselves while tuning into the context of the organization and the moment. Such figures are in short supply. Goffee and Jones cite former British prime minister Tony Blair as an exemplar of the breed, someone who was able to tailor his leadership behavior to fit in with an organization – the Labour Party – while being true to himself.

It all depends.

Resources

Fred Fiedler, *Leadership* (General Learning Press, 1971).

Paul Hersey and Ken Blanchard, *Management of Organizational Behavior* (Prentice Hall, 1969).

We interviewed Warren Bennis many times. Some of the interviews can be found in our book *Leadership: Organizational Success through Leadership* (McGraw Hill, 2013).

Rob Goffee and Gareth Jones' work is best accessed in *Why Should Anyone Be Led By You?* (Harvard Business Press, 2006).

The only way is ethics   #6

One of the most impressive companies we have encountered is the family-owned foods business, Mars. It began life in 1911 when Franklin C. Mars made the first Mars candies in his kitchen in Tacoma, Washington. The business was later run by Forrest Mars Jr. and the family is still actively involved.

Mars is built around adherence to five principles – quality, responsibility, mutuality, efficiency and freedom. The principles are available in book form and are given to all associates. Of course, many companies have similar statements of what matters to them – values, missions, goals and so on fill the flimsy walls of corporate buildings throughout the world. Most are as decorative as they are generic.

Countering such cynicism, Pamela Mars-Wright injects a note of realism:

> It would be unfair to say that other companies don't exercise their principles. They do. I don't by any stretch of the imagination want to say that Mars is so much better than other companies. You can always find things that you talk about that you don't practice as well as you should. At the end of the day, businesses are still run by human beings so, as a result, we make mistakes, but we really do practice our principles and expect our associates to practice them.

The five principles are the cornerstone of Mars' culture and management. Associates new to the business are embraced through an 'Essence of Mars' course, which aims to provide the foundation for early success in their careers at Mars. Training courses are available globally, in twenty-two languages, and aim to support associate development and understanding of how to apply Mars' five principles to their work and business decisions. More than 40 percent of Mars associates every year participate in learning programs worldwide through Mars University. This is equivalent to 400,000 learning hours every year.

Mars (with annual sales of $33 billion) is proof that the greatest leadership has an ethical element. Always.

At the end of the 1980s we spent an afternoon with the great management thinker Peter Drucker. He recounted stories of encounters with Sigmund Freud when he was a child in Vienna, coming to London to work with *The Economist*, his first break working with General Motors when he settled in the United States. He told us of his love of Trollope and of rereading Jane Austen every year to remind himself what great writing is. And, talking about his books, he observed that there was one big book which everyone in the business world aspires to write: *How to Make a Million and Still Go to Heaven*.

Drucker's joking suggestion of a book title has a serious point. Greatness and goodness lie at the heart of many of the discussions about how best to manage, lead and shape organizations.

At times the two appear mutually exclusive. Business greatness in terms of financial results is regularly achieved at the expense of any notion of ethical behavior. Companies can appear, feel and be amoral, sometimes pursuing unethical means to achieve their commercial ends.

At the same time, we have all encountered organizations whose pursuit of goodness, a moral agenda, has limited their commercial achievements.

Truth be told, even in this age of Corporate Social Responsibility, employee engagement and much more, the number of companies achieving commercial success through enlightened working practices and policies within clear ethical guidelines remains painfully small in number. Think of some names of the corporate great and good and they are likely to number less than the fingers of one hand.

By example   #7

In 1982, a psychopath put cyanide into some Tylenol capsules. Eight people died. In response, Johnson & Johnson withdrew the product in its entirety from store shelves. A total of 31 million bottles were returned to J&J. This cost J&J $100 million. (Contrast this with when Perrier found traces of benzene in its products. It only recalled a small number from the North American market. The fallout was far greater than the original problem.)

Then J&J accepted responsibility – though it was clear that it hadn't actually done anything wrong. J&J's response was candid. It opted for full cooperation with the media immediately. Later the company offered to exchange Tylenol capsules – which were the contaminated product – for Tylenol tablets. Many more millions of dollars were spent in doing so.

Key to this was the behavior of J&J CEO Jim Burke. The Irish-American emerged as an honest, straight-talking, highly responsible executive. He personally toured one TV program after another to take responsibility and keep people up-to-date. J&J's media response won plaudit after plaudit. 'What Johnson & Johnson executives have done is communicate the message that the company is candid, contrite and compassionate, committed to solving the murders and protecting the public,' noted the *Washington Post*.

Tylenol remains a bestselling over-the-counter drug. J&J invested heavily in restoring it to its previous position – it had 37 percent of the over-the-counter painkiller market. 'It will take time, it will take money, and it will be very difficult; but we consider it a moral imperative, as well as good business, to restore Tylenol to its pre-eminent position,' said Jim Burke. Thanks to the company's responsible response, its sales quickly recovered.

Leading in such a crisis is clearly difficult in the extreme. It is interesting that the fact that J&J had a 'Credo' with clearly delineated standards of behavior made the crisis easier to handle. Burke had led a program to revisit the Credo and update it for the 1980s, making it a real and influential document which had a direct effect on people's behavior. Over ten years, J&J had reconsidered the Credo. The Tylenol crisis brought its values into sharp relief. Instead of bringing in a contingency plan, the company carried on expressing the same principles and values. What the public saw was genuine principled leadership.

Crises as awful as Tylenol rarely happen. J&J's decisive response met the challenge. It reacted coolly and positively to crisis. It set up a crisis management team, identified the key people who needed to be involved, and limited numbers of spokesmen and women. Most of all, Burke gave a lead.

Any one can hold the helm when the sea is calm,' as Pubilius Syrus noted many centuries ago. He remains right. When the going gets tough, leaders get to work by setting an example.

Konosuke Matsushita, creator of the Japanese corporate empire which bore his name, advocated business with a conscience. This was manifested in his paternalistic employment practices. During a recession early in its life the company did not make any people redundant. This cemented loyalty. 'It's not enough to work conscientiously. No matter what kind of job, you should think of yourself as being completely in charge of and responsible for your own work,' he said, going on to describe how he approached his work: 'Big things and little things are my job. Middle-level arrangements can be delegated.' He also explained the role of the leader in more cryptic style: 'The tail trails the head. If the head moves fast, the tail will keep up the same pace. If the head is sluggish, the tail will droop.'

Behind such aphorisms lies profound leadership truth. At a soccer match we encountered a burger seller who had 'Team Leader' on his name badge. Emboldened by beer we asked what leadership meant to him. 'Two words,' he immediately replied, barely pausing for breath. 'By example.' We returned to our seats stunned by the brilliant power of his response. We know plenty of business leaders and thinkers in the subject who would fail to answer with such speed, confidence and authenticity.

One of the most inspiring stories of leading by ethical example is that of Aaron Feuerstein of the American company Malden Mills. In 1995 he decided to keep his business open after a major fire. He kept the workforce of 2,400 people on the payroll out of his own personal savings.

Malden Mills was already a pretty unusual company prior to 11 December 1995. In an age of diminishing loyalty and relentless downsizing, it stood for traditional corporate values. Loyal employees worked alongside trusting management. Customer retention and employee retention both registered a staggering 95 percent. The company, based in Lawrence, Massachusetts, had remained steadfastly – some said foolishly – loyal to its home base. Founded in 1906, it moved to Lawrence in 1956 rather than following its competitors and many more textile companies in their migration down south.

Malden Mills stayed stoically put. Its loyalty seemed misplaced when, in the early 1970s, it made a disastrous move into fake fur. By 1980 it was in Chapter 11. Malden Mills struck back with the development of Polartec, a lightweight fleece which proved more successful – and tasteful – than fake fur. By 1995 it had sales of $400 million.

Then a fire ripped through its factories leaving over a dozen people hospitalized and the company, it seemed, in ruins.

Malden Mills chief, Aaron Feuerstein, the grandson of the company's founder, immediately announced that – with no production capacity and no immediate hope of producing anything – he would continue to pay the company's 2,400 employees and pay their healthcare insurance. It was estimated that paying the company's employees for 90 days and their healthcare for 180 days cost Feuerstein $10 million.

'Most people would've been happy at their seventieth birthday to take the insurance money and go to Florida, but I don't want to do that,' Feuerstein said. It appeared like bad business at the time even though it was highly moral.

In the end, Malden Mills was back to virtually full capacity within ninety days. A total of $15 million was invested in a new infrastructure. The committed and grateful workforce worked so well that productivity and quality shot up – before the fire 6 to 7 percent of the company's production was 'off quality'; this reduced to 2 percent after the fire. Feuerstein said the company's employees paid him back nearly tenfold.

And the lessons from this? First, ethics come naturally or not at all. Feuerstein considered it the natural thing to do. 'Fifty years ago it would have been considered very natural for a CEO, if his plant burned down, to rebuild it and to worry about his people,' he lamented.

The second lesson is that (somewhat surprisingly perhaps) ethics pay. Feuerstein's act was one of loyalty, honesty and morality. But, it brought paybacks – President Clinton was among those paying homage to Feuerstein by inviting him to Washington. 'I always thought that perhaps in the long run [my employees] would return to me a quality product that would make Malden Mills continue to excel. But I never dreamed there would be any short-term advantage,' he said.

The reality is that organizations live with communities and vice versa. Only Gordon Gekko would believe that companies and communities can be clinically separated. 'One of the great lessons I learned these past few months is how fundamental our businesses are to the survival and health of our communities,' said Feuerstein. Leadership is driven by and for communities.

Leaders change things   #8

'Leadership produces change. That is its primary function,' observes Harvard Business School's John Kotter. Former CEO, Larry Bossidy puts it like this: 'The leader's job is to help everyone see that the platform is burning, whether the flames are apparent or not. The process of change begins when people decide to take the flames seriously and manage by fact, and that means a brutal understanding of reality. You need to find out what the reality is so that you know what needs changing.'

Leaders are rarely recruited to maintain the status quo. When they are it is often a recipe for disaster. Probably the best example of this is the recruitment of David Moyes to follow the hugely successful tenure of Sir Alex Ferguson as manager of the soccer club Manchester United. Moyes was the continuity candidate, someone in the same image as Ferguson – dour, Scottish, fiercely committed and intense. From the moment he took the job, Moyes was caught in a no man's land of trying to put his own stamp on the club while maintaining things as they had been. The past won.

While change is integral to the job description of any leader, it is fraught with difficulty. We have worked closely with CEOs who have failed to last the course. All were bright, ambitious, hard working and obvious people to take up senior leadership jobs.

The first became CEO of a major professional organization. He wanted to drag it into the twenty-first century and developed a smart strategy to do so. Every time we visited his office, he went through his presentation of the strategy. It was highly convincing. But that was in

Powerpoint. In reality, he had completely underestimated the reluctance of people to willingly embrace change. However brilliant the strategy, the people in the organization needed time to learn to trust the new CEO and to understand the strategy as an opportunity rather than a threat. The CEO carried on regardless, irritating people, attempting to shake things up and then being left shaking his head as nothing happened. He lasted six months.

At another firm we worked with a CEO who was hugely impressive. He knew the organization inside out, had worked throughout the world for it and appeared a thoroughly likeable person. So far, so good.

He then hatched a similarly ambitious strategy and set about implementing it. He also wrote a book about being a CEO. We imagine that didn't endear him to people. Again, to mix metaphors, feathers were ruffled and he bit the corporate dust.

Change is never easy. Never. Research repeatedly bemoans the high failure rate of change initiatives. And there is no sign that the failure rate is declining. But, the truth is that change is what leaders do. Indeed, leadership could be pithily defined as being the catalyst for change. Leadership enables change and changing things is core to any understanding of leadership. While management is concerned with maximizing the efficiency of what exists, leadership is concerned with bringing about quantum leaps in performance by changing how things are thought about and done.

The Harvard professor Rosabeth Moss Kanter has looked at the leaders who excel at dealing with change – what she labels the 'change masters' – and has also researched turnaround leadership in detail. Kanter says that 'the most important things a leader can bring to a changing organization are passion, conviction, and confidence in others'.

Based on studies of several turnarounds, she suggests that information and relationships are crucial elements. A turnaround leader must facilitate a psychological change of attitudes and behavior before organizational recovery can take place. She identifies four essential components of the turnaround process: promoting dialogue, engendering respect, sparking collaboration and inspiring initiative.

Kanter also notes that a great change leader remembers to reward, recognize and celebrate the accomplishments of the people involved in the change process. Make everyone a hero, she says. Because, as she points out, 'There is no limit to how much recognition you can provide, and it is often free. Recognition brings the change cycle to its logical conclusion, but it also motivates people to attempt change again.'

Recognition can be as big or small an issue as you make it. The executive coach Marshall Goldsmith makes the point that simply saying thank you is probably the most efficient form of recognition. It is remarkable how low expectations are in this regard. (Witness the Hawthorne research in the 1930s where production went up simply because employees thought that supervisors were paying attention to their needs.)

Recognition is an entry point. As Rosabeth Moss Kanter suggests, leading change can never be a simple matter of forcibly corralling people in a particular direction. People have to want to head in that direction; they have to want to change.

This is what Michael Jarrett, a professor at INSEAD, calls 'readiness for change'. 'Readiness for change applies at the philosophical level – being open to and prepared to embrace change; but it also applies at the practical level,' he says:

Readiness applies to those organizations that have developed a set of core dynamic and internal capabilities that allow them to adapt when faced by external demands. It is the precursor to those organizations that gain strategic agility. Basically, successful change is a function of how well an organization's internal capabilities – its management capacity, culture, processes, resources and people – match the requirements of its external environment, the marketplace.

Change is a match-making process. The leader has to have an appetite for change. The organization needs to be ready for change – and, if not, the leader has to nurture its readiness for change. And the organization has to change in the right way to meet the needs of its time, its marketplace, its reality. Are you ready?

Resources

Rosabeth Moss Kanter's best known book is *The Change Masters* (Simon & Schuster, 1983). Also recommended is *Confidence* (Three Rivers Press, 2006).

Michael Jarrett's ideas are captured in *Changeability* (Prentice Hall, 2009).

Leaders question #9

The CEO of a high-tech company told us of how his wife despaired of his habit of talking to strangers when he saw how they were using technology:

> My wife says that I'm almost politically incorrect when I meet people, because I ask questions that I should not ask. But I believe that if you are interested in how people use technology, you should ask; and even if the way I do this is sometimes politically incorrect or embarrassing, people will find a way to deal with me, so, what's the problem? How people now use technology to reprogram their lives (for example, how people easily used their phones or laptops to keep track of plane delays due to the Icelandic volcano eruption) is fascinating to me. It's always fascinated me, and I think I will continue to find it fascinating.

The ability to ask questions is something leaders repeatedly refer to when we talk with them. This is especially true during transitions in role. 'I think the questions you ask are always the most difficult thing; answering the question is somehow easy if you've found the right question. There are a hundred wrong questions for you to grab onto and completely waste your time with, but if at the beginning you can find the right question …' Chris Gibson-Smith, then chairman of the London Stock Exchange, told us.

In some organizations the ability to ask the right questions is ingrained in the culture. At the design firm IDEO the culture is shaped by what is called 'design thinking'. This is an approach to solving problems which argues that you should initially invest time in framing the question well, because if you frame the question badly the only certainty is that you're going to get bad answers. Typically companies underinvest in getting the question right.

'Design thinking is really about applying design methodologies to a much broader set of challenges in the world,' explains IDEO CEO Tim Brown. 'I have never yet seen an interesting creative idea that didn't come from an interesting creative question. And so you might think about what are the kinds of questions that you can ask in an organization that inspire people to think differently, to question things in new ways, to discover new possibilities.'

Tim Brown points to a survey of 1,500 CEOs which asked what was the most important quality for dealing with a complex world. Creativity was ranked top. 'In today's uncertain, volatile, rapidly changing world, creative leadership may just be the most important form of leadership there is,' says Brown. 'We think of leadership as about having the right answers but if you really want to unleash the creativity of an organization, that's not the most important thing at all. In fact it can actually be an impediment if you think that your job as a leader is to have the best ideas.'

Creative leadership requires that leaders develop a sense of purpose in the organization, ask great questions and create a great stage for others to perform on. 'If you do those things well, you really do have a chance of unlocking not only your own creative potential but the creative potential of all those people that you lead or that are around you, and that can be a pretty powerful way of making change happen in the world,' argues Tim Brown.

The ability to ask questions depends on the willingness of people within any organizations to have honest and transparent communications. This is often not the case. Politics, machinations, ambition, greed and much more can get in the way of honest and upfront communication.

It is reassuring when you encounter this sort of transparency. We talked to Ben Slater, CEO of the London-based growth consultancy Bow

& Arrow. Bow & Arrow's values are displayed on the walls. They go beyond the usual corporate platitudes. Says Slater:

We have a value which is "we say what we really think and feel" and that means often having the uncomfortable conversation, the direct, difficult chat with a client to say, look, you haven't got sponsorship here, we haven't even met your CEO let alone had the CEO tell the business about the importance of this project, or we haven't been to the factory, or you've not aligned this person. So we're incredibly forthcoming about where the problems are starting to arise and capturing them and flagging them and making sure they're dealt with.

He thanks being brought up by two lawyers for his insistence on straight-talking honesty.

Taking soundings from people in the organization is especially important for the new leader. Sally Tennant, CEO of Kleinwort Benson Bank, recounts her preparation for taking over as CEO:

I spent a lot of time before I came reading about the business, reading board reports, meeting some of the top team and thinking about the issues. And, in my first four weeks, I had around seventy one-on-one, or one-on-two, meetings in the UK and the Channel Islands, all lasting from an hour to an hour and a half. I pretty much asked everyone all the same questions so I then had a level playing field.

At each meeting, the new CEO took handwritten notes. Her aim, she explains, was to better understand each individual, their responsibilities and how she could support them. Initially the conversation was restricted to individual areas of responsibility. Next it moved onto the business generally. Did they understand the strategy? Was it being pursued? Was it likely to get the organization to where it wanted to be? Then Tennant went into the organizational culture. What was good and bad about the way things were done? Were there any skeletons in the organizational cupboard likely to come toppling out? And where were the quick wins, the immediate changes which could make a powerful difference?

'I asked everybody, if you were me, what would you focus on? What are the key issues?' says Tennant.

> It's very interesting, if you do that across the organization. You start very, very quickly, building a picture of where the strengths and weaknesses are. So, my objective in the first four or five weeks was to get a picture as quickly as possible about what the key challenges were. I also wanted to get to meet as many people and gain their respect, because if you're going to come in and change things, it's easier to do so from the basis of people wanting to change. I also wanted to see where the talent lay, where the gaps were, in order to put together a plan.

Sally Tennant suggests that connecting directly with people actually creates its own momentum. There is a feeling of things changing simply by beginning a dialogue. 'I have created momentum by spending time with people, but not just internally. I went to see some of our clients within the first five or six weeks. In a service business, particularly in financial services, I think it's incredibly important for a CEO to have client contact, to understand client needs.' Without dialogue with customers and employees, leaders exist in a vacuum. And those who fail to connect will simply fail to make the transition to leadership.

Resources

The best book on IDEO's approach is Tom Kelley and Jonathan Littman's *The Art of Innovation* (Currency/Doubleday, 2001).

The prince of leadership

#10

The twenty-first century has more than its fair share of self-improvement books. Publications promising the secrets of time management, stunning presentations and interviews fill countless bookshelves, not to mention the blogs, tweets and much more. Just over five hundred years ago, the first publication of its type was produced. Niccolo Machiavelli's *The Prince* is the sixteenth-century equivalent of Dale Carnegie's *How to Win Friends and Influence People*. Embedded beneath details of Alexander VI's tribulations lie a ready supply of aphorisms and insights which are, perhaps sadly, as appropriate to many of today's leaders and organizations as they were half a millennium ago. (Indeed, Antony Jay's 1970 book, *Management and Machiavelli* developed the comparisons.)

Machiavelli (1469–1527) served as an official in the Florentine government. During fourteen years as Secretary of the Second Chancery, he became known as the 'Florentine Secretary' and served on nearly thirty foreign missions. His work brought him into contact with some of Europe's most influential ministers and government representatives. His chief diplomatic triumph occurred when Florence obtained the surrender of Pisa in 1509.

Machiavelli's career came to an end in 1512 when the Medicis returned to power. He was then exiled from the city and later accused of being involved in a plot against the government. For this he was imprisoned and tortured on the rack. He then retired to a farm outside

Florence and began a successful writing career, with books on politics as well as plays and a history of Florence.

His ideas still resonate. 'Like the leaders Machiavelli sought to defend, some executives tend to see themselves as the natural rulers in whose hands organizations can be safely entrusted,' says psychologist Robert Sharrock of consultants YSC. 'Theories abound on their motivation. Is it a defensive reaction against failure or a need for predictability through complete control? The effect of the power-driven Machiavellian manager is usually plain to see.'

'It is unnecessary for a prince to have all the good qualities I have enumerated, but it is very necessary to appear to have them,' Machiavelli advises, adding the suggestion that it is useful 'to be a great pretender and dissembler'. But *The Prince* goes beyond such helpful presentational hints. Like all great books, it offers something for everyone. Take Machiavelli on managing change: 'There is nothing more difficult to take in hand, more perilous to conduct, or more uncertain in its success, than to take the lead in the introduction of a new order of things.' Or on sustaining motivation: 'He ought above all things to keep his men well organized and drilled, to follow incessantly the chase.'

Machiavelli even has advice for executives acquiring companies in other countries:

> But when states are acquired in a country differing in language, customs or laws, there are difficulties, and good fortune and great energy are needed to hold them, and one of the greatest and most real helps would be that he who has acquired them should go and reside there ... Because if one is on the spot, disorders are seen as they spring up, and one can quickly remedy them; but if one is not at hand, they are heard of only when they are great, and then one can no longer remedy them.

Leaders throughout the world will be able to identify with Machiavelli's analysis.

Machiavelli is at his best in discussing leadership. Success, he says, is not down to luck or genius, but 'happy shrewdness'. In Machiavelli's hands, this is a euphemism. Elsewhere, he advises 'a Prince ought to have no other aim or thought, nor select anything else for his study, than war and its rules and discipline; for this is the sole art that belongs to him who rules'.

The Prince also examines the perils facing the self-made leader when they reach the dizzy heights: 'Those who solely by good fortune become princes from being private citizens have little trouble in rising, but much in keeping atop; they have not any difficulties on the way up, because they fly, but they have many when they reach the summit'.

Above all, Machiavelli is the champion of leadership through cunning and intrigue, the triumph of force over reason. An admirer of Cesare Borgia, Machiavelli had a dismal view of human nature. Unfortunately, as he sagely points out, history has repeatedly proved that a combination of being armed to the teeth and devious is more likely to allow you to achieve your objectives. It is all very well being good, says Machiavelli, but the leader 'should know how to enter into evil when necessity commands'. Beware!

Resources

Machiavelli's *The Prince* is worth seeking out in any bookstore. Put it on your bookshelves and, at the very least, people will begin to wonder.

The humility of leaders   #11

Humility is not a word often associated with modern leaders. Indeed, a humble leader is almost a contradiction in terms. But it shouldn't be.

'A leader should be humble. A leader should be able to communicate with his people. A leader is someone who walks out in front of his people, but he doesn't get too far out in front, to where he can't hear their footsteps,' observed Tommy Lasorda, a player and manager of the LA Dodgers.

The great Indian-born business thinker C. K. Prahalad was a strong advocate of leadership humility. Talking with C. K. shortly before his premature death in 2010, he discussed leadership and the necessary characteristics of the new generation of leaders. 'I think humility is a good start,' he said:

> I think we got to a point where if you want to be a leader you had to be arrogant. No. First, leadership is about hope, leadership is about change and leadership is about the future. And if you start with those three premises, I want leaders who are willing to listen because the future is not clear. People who can only tell you about the past because there's certainty about the past are not showing leadership. With the future, there's not much certainty, so you have to listen and bring in multiple perspectives.

C. K. was a naturally humble man and one who listened. On a number of occasions we filmed interviews with him. At the end of every one he talked to the cameramen and sound engineers to see what they thought. He wasn't overly concerned about whether the lighting had shown up some physical blemish or whether his tie was straight. What concerned him was whether what he had said had made sense to them. If he had made them pay attention and if they had understood his arguments, then he was doing his job.

Like any natural teacher, C. K. had a gift for storytelling, of using apt and easily understood metaphors and comparisons. This is how he explained his take on leadership when we spoke to him:

> Let me use a metaphor. I look at good leaders as sheepdogs. Good sheepdogs have to follow three rules. One, you can bark a lot, but don't bite. Number two, you have to be behind, you cannot be ahead of the sheep. Number three, you must know where to go and don't lose the sheep.
>
> If you think about leadership it's about consensus building, because when you have stakeholders, if you have to worry about co-creation, you must listen and you must build consensus. You can have multiple conversations, but it's equal to bark a lot but don't bite. People who tell you things which are different may be more valuable than people who agree with you because, like the old saying, if you can bark yourself, why have a dog? If all the people agree with you then why have so many people? You already know the answer. So dissent is an integral part of understanding what the new leader will look like.
>
> And you must have a point of view of the future. You cannot lead unless you have a point of view. And most leaders do not have a point of view or if they have it they don't express it clearly. Increasing shareholder wealth cannot be a point of view about the future. It's incidental to doing the right things.

C. K. Prahalad's ideas chime with our times – especially in the wake of the financial crisis and resulting global depression. They are also echoed by the work of Jim Collins, author of the 2001 bestseller *Good to Great* (and co-author of the 1994 bestseller *Built to Last*). Collins champions a combination of selflessness, humility and iron will. These leaders are usually 'quiet leaders' and not the larger-than-life figures, the charismatic heroes much feted by Wall Street and the City. For leadership, humility is the final frontier.

Collins introduced a new term to the leadership lexicon to describe this type of leader – Level 5 leadership. Going through the skills at each level, Level 1 is about individual capability, someone who uses their knowledge and talent to contribute to the organization. Level 2 is about team skills and working with a group effectively. At Level 3 a person exhibits managerial competence, they can get people organized towards shared goals. Level 4 is leadership in the conventional non-Jim Collins sense, they articulate vision and stimulate performance.

At the top level is Level 5. Level 5 is great, while Level 4 leaders are merely good.

According to Collins, humility is a key ingredient of Level 5 leadership. His simple formula is Humility + Will = Level 5. 'Level 5 leaders are a study in duality', notes Collins, 'modest and willful, shy and fearless.' Level 5 leaders display a number of distinct attributes. Although instrumental in achieving great results, they never brag about it, preferring to avoid the limelight.

They are resolute about the organization's objectives but do not motivate through force of personality in a charismatic sense, but through demonstrating principles and standards. While panning for sustained success they are happy and even keen to organize an effective successor.

When thing go wrong, they do not pass the buck. Instead they are happy to shoulder the burden of responsibility. And when things go well, then are quick to praise others and acknowledge the contributions of their team.

Change your perspective of leadership to adopt a Level 5 view of the world and the talent map of the organization changes. Level 5 leaders can be found inside most organizations. The problem is the cult of the heroic leader that permeates the business world and much further afield.

The questions for the leader raised by the issue of humility are many and varied. In the end they can be distilled down to whether they get a buzz from the achievements of others or solely from their own.

Resources

C. K. Prahalad's most important book is *The Fortune at the Bottom of the Pyramid* (Wharton Press, 2004). It helped reconfigure views of the poorest people in emerging markets.

It is worth reading Jim Collins' *Good To Great: Why Some Companies Make The Leap... And Others Don't* (Harper Business, 2001) and seeking out his *Harvard Business Review* article 'Level 5 Leadership: The Triumph of Humility and Fierce Resolve' (January, 2001).

Coffee culture

Recently we were at a meeting at a major international bank. We were meeting with one of the bank's directors to talk about a potential sponsorship deal. We made our way through reception and security up to the thirtieth floor where the panoramic views of London were breathtaking.

Then in came the banker we were meeting. After the usual greetings, he asked if we would like a cup of tea or coffee though, he added, 'I should tell you that the coffee is truly awful here'. We paused and declined.

Thinking back there were a couple of other organizations we had visited over the years where people had said something similar. Their coffee was also a drink only for the truly desperate.

A storm in a coffee cup perhaps, but such small things communicate very strong messages. The banker talked exhaustively about how the bank was changing its culture to one of greater transparency and so on. Engagement and excellence were alluded to.

And yet the bank couldn't even offer a good cup of coffee to visitors – or its own staff. Of course, it could be interpreted as sensible care of its finances, a bank unwilling to throw money around on half decent coffee. Or of Presbyterian professionalism, an organization unwilling to underwrite peripheries.

But that is not what we thought. We looked around at the beautifully appointed and hugely expensive offices, and the well-remunerated banker sitting in front of us, and thought it odd that for all the talk of excellence and so on, the first communication we had had was about a low-quality product which the banker and the organization were happy to have on offer to staff and visitors.

What did this say about the company's culture and its attitude to its employees and visitors? Our conclusion: not much.

We thought back to other experiences where our welcome was tepid and unfriendly. Once we flew across the Atlantic for a meeting at which we weren't offered a drink at all – it was a two-hour meeting, first thing in the morning. We can recall a handful of other such occasions. The thing is we remember them, the people and the organizations. Bad experiences – and cultures – stick in the memory.

And then, at our recent caffeine-free meeting at the bank, to make matters worse, the banker started to tell us what a hectic time it had been for him lately, how working for a bank was incredibly demanding and time consuming. He would, we thought, have benefitted from some decently caffeinated and drinkable coffee. And we have regularly encountered such lamentations, people telling us how hard they are working and what a hectic organization/industry they are in.

This may well be true. The banker did look slightly unhealthy and frazzled. But there are a number of assumptions here. First, we often have the sense that people wish us to be impressed by the hectic, packed nature of their schedules, a kind of diary envy. Truth be told, we are desperately unimpressed by people who tell us they work every hour of the day and have meetings scheduled to cover every waking minute. Is this efficient? We doubt it. Is it leadership? Most definitely not.

The second assumption at work here is that people who tell you how hard they are working are assuming that they work harder than you do. They may well be, but most people are working harder and longer. It doesn't matter if you are sweeping the street or running a multinational, work is demanding and draining.

We left the bank shaking our heads. As we discussed the meeting over a reviving cup of coffee, we contemplated the lessons it offered. Obviously, the secret to success is not simply a matter of serving drinkable coffee and remembering not to tell people how hard you are working. The starting point of success is not to accept mediocrity. Once it has been accepted, second rate becomes the default expectation of the organization. And it starts with small things, such as the coffee on offer. That's why companies such as Google offer great and free food and drink to all employees. An army – and every other organization – marches on its stomach.

The second thing is to listen and think of other people. No one really cares if you work twenty hours a day – especially if you are a highly paid banker. Success requires that you tune into your audience. What do they think? What is on their agenda? Ask them and then pass the chocolate to shake on their perfectly prepared cappuccino.

The real thing #13

Imagine you are CEO of a major corporation. The information you have suggests major problems lie ahead. Sales are falling. Market share is under threat. Talking to the world, do you honestly express your serious concerns about the business or do you put a protective gloss on reality? The latter is virtually always the answer.

Faced with a patient, a doctor is more likely to offer an optimistic scenario than a negative one. When a politician meets a voter in the flesh, many voters express a deep commitment to voting for the politician in front of them. Often they fail to carry this through.

Leaders tailor their messages all the time. They don't need spin doctors; it is human nature. Truth bends. This is not deception – well, usually not – but a kind of leadership artifice, realization that leadership is a show.

Think of how a teacher grabs a class's attention. Think of how you might take a meeting by storm. Think of how a leader enters the room and raises the atmosphere. Leadership may not be show business, but the leader tends to wear some greasepaint.

There is no denying the theatrical element necessary to succeed as a leader. 'The example I use with the executives that I work with is a Broadway or a West End play. People in a show do not say, oh my foot hurts, I don't feel too good today, I'm in a bad mood. Why? Because it is show time. I tell the executives that the kid on the stage is making 2 percent of what you're making. If they can go out there, night after night after night, and be a professional, then so can you,' says the executive coach Marshall Goldsmith.

How a leader behaves makes a difference. If they are miserable, their mood is infectious. A casual offhand remark can spread through the organization like wildfire. Every moment. Every move. Every word and every communication has an audience and has an impact on that audience.

But, and this is a considerable impediment, at the same time the loudest leadership chorus of recent years has championed the case of the authentic leader. The torch bearers for the idea include former CEO of Medtronic, Bill George, and business school academics such as Rob Goffee and Liz Mellon (author of *Inside the Leader's Mind*).

With authentic leadership, the best leaders make the most of the qualities they already possess. They trade on their strengths and understand their weaknesses. Authentic leadership is definitely not about adopting the styles or traits of other successful leaders. It is about honestly and consistently being yourself.

This is all very well, but counters most of the received wisdom of recent decades which has been about learning from and emulating the traits of the leadership greats. From Churchill to Jobs, leaders have been entreated to watch, learn and copy.

'We realize that the missing ingredients in corporations are ethical leaders committed to building authentic organizations for the long term,' said Bill George. 'We need authentic leaders, people of the highest integrity, committed to building enduring organizations. We need leaders who have a deep sense of purpose and are true to their core values. We need leaders with the courage to build their companies to meet the needs of all their stakeholders, and who recognize the importance of their service to society.'

According to George, authentic leaders: understand their purpose, and have the passion for that purpose that comes from being highly motivated by their work; have solid values, of which integrity should be one, and practice those values testing themselves in different situations; should be able to lead with their heart, treating followers with compassion, and firing up employees to achieve great things; must forge common purpose and build a sense of connectedness so that they develop enduring relationships with, and inspire loyalty and trust from, their employees; and authentic leadership requires a high degree of self-discipline – this means dealing with stress effectively and maintaining wellbeing.

This is all well and good. Authenticity feels like the right thing to do. It feels good. The trouble is that it sits uncomfortably with the inauthentic nature of a great deal of necessary leadership behavior. Leaders have to appear unworried even if they know that disaster is looming – because if their smile breaks, disaster will arrive all the quicker.

And then there is the 'show time' element. Some amount of artifice, of behaving counter to your habitual behavior, is often necessary to communicate and engage with people.

For leaders this is one of the great dilemmas: how can they square manifestly inauthentic behavior with the need to be themselves? In the end their most authentic thing may be their response to this question.

Resources

Bill George's ideas are best expressed in *Authentic Leadership: Rediscovering the Secrets to Creating Lasting Value* (Jossey-Bass, 2003) and his co-authored article 'Discovering Your Authentic Leadership' (*Harvard Business Review*, February, 2007).

Returning home

It is difficult sometimes to go into situations with your eyes wide open. You make judgments, leap to assumptions, remember old prejudices and snippets of probably incorrect information. And so it was when we went on a business trip to Istanbul.

Our previous visits to Turkey had been decades before. We remembered dusty streets, wonderful food and a country which the brightest and best people usually left in search of employment.

Our trip was to visit the Turkish communications company Turkcell. Turkey is the meeting point of continents, the fulcrum of civilizations and empires, a nation with trade and commerce in its bloodstream, so it came as a surprise when we were doing some background research that the country had a mixed record with technology. It was a late convert to the printing press, for instance – that technology took two hundred years to make the journey from Holland. Centuries later, there was a similar lack of enthusiasm for the telephone.

The phone line installed in 1881 between the old Post Office building and Yeni Cami Post Office in Soğukçeşme was the first telephone line in Turkey. Others followed, but development came to an abrupt halt when Sultan Abdul Hamid II made it clear that he did not much like the telephone. He saw its potential for fermenting whispered traitorous discussions. Phone lines were removed by order of the Sultan in 1886, and his veto remained in place until 1908.

Arrive today in Turkey and such laggardly embrace of technology feels like ancient history. Past experiences and preconceptions are quickly forgotten. This is one of the world's fastest-growing economies. Turn on your mobile phone and there is the reassuring sight of five full bars. Reception is good. Using broadband, the full extent of the nation's high-tech present quickly becomes clear. While other nations struggle with the infrastructure requirements of superfast broadband, the Turks enjoy some of the fastest broadband speeds in the world.

The internet speed in Diyarbakir in south-eastern Turkey is four times faster than in Paris and more than twice as fast as the London and Berlin speeds. According to the OECD, Turkey's online speeds are only matched by those of Slovenia, Japan and Sweden.

In 1994, Turkcell started the country's first GSM network, and signed a twenty-five-year GSM license with the Turkish government in 1998. By 2013, it had acquired 35.1 million subscribers in Turkey and had a domestic market share of 51.5 percent. Half of Turkey's population are now Turkcell customers. But Turkcell's success is more significant and impressive than simply having a captive home market. In fact, competition is fierce – from Vodafone and Turk Telekom among others – and genuine.

The speed with which Turkcell has grown is indicative of its technological and commercial intent. It also owes something to the fervor of its then CEO Sureyya Ciliv.

Tall, shaven-headed Sureyya Ciliv cut an eye-catching figure as he walked around Turkcell HQ in Istanbul. His story is a compelling one. As part of a pilot project funded by the Ford Foundation, the young Ciliv was one of a carefully selected group of ninety-six students who were chosen annually to be sent to a boarding school just outside of Ankara.

The focus of his education was on science. Students each had their own microscopes – an unheard of thing at that time. Each day they watched videos of leaders in their fields teaching. 'The school didn't care where pupils came from. You didn't get in because of your parents knowing someone. The result was there was a huge mix of people – Kurds, Muslims, Jews. It gave me a respect for, interest in and love of knowledge and science.'

This educational melting pot gave Ciliv an interest in electronics and computers. He won a scholarship to the University of Michigan. 'I studied and studied and studied,' he recalls. 'At times I had 25 cents left in my pocket, but I wouldn't spend it because I didn't want to be penniless.' From there, he did an MBA at Harvard Business School and developed an interest in technology and entrepreneurship. 'At Harvard 50 percent of the grade was related to class discussion. So, you needed a good story and to be able to tell it. I realized that someone who was good at arguing their case effectively could get their way and that marketing can be based on analysis. I improved my technical analysis, decision analysis and so on. I was a big fan of optimization; for me it was the meaning of life.'

He listened to Bill Gates and Steve Jobs speak at the school. When the chairman and CEO of IBM, Frank Carey, came to speak, Ciliv stood up and asked how he came to be the number one man at what was then the world's number one company. Carey replied that he had always been ready. Sureyya Ciliv took this as his watchword.

He had eleven job offers on leaving Harvard, but took the one with the lowest salary – $29,000 joining a start-up rather than a six-figure salary as an investment banker. He then initiated his own start-up before joining Microsoft in Turkey. He credits Microsoft as a great education – 'I'm really a student of Microsoft rather than Harvard Business School. I'm still learning, but Microsoft taught me about execution in the field. They took the message to people and then fine tuned it quickly.'

'I was a bit different to the typical Microsoft employee,' Ciliv recalls. 'I defined my mission as using Microsoft's resources to contribute to Turkey.' He became head of sales for the Microsoft Office and was then approached by a headhunter working to fill the CEO position at Turkcell.

'I wasn't very interested initially,' Ciliv admits. 'The headhunter said that Turkcell was a star company in Turkey and was entering a new phase with intensifying competition. He said that the team needed a captain.' Sureyya Ciliv returned home.

As we took our leave of Ciliv and Turkcell, what remained with us was a sense of entrepreneurial energy and vigor. The company's success was not about the technology and broadband speeds – impressive though they are – but about the people and the leadership.

Crucibles for leaders   #15

For Nelson Mandela it was Robben Island. For John McCain it was Vietnam. There is a point in the lives of leaders, a moment when the leader makes the grade, when they leap from management to leadership, from team member to leader. For the leadership theorist Warren Bennis that moment came when he was the youngest infantry officer in the European theater of operations during World War II. This experience was what Bennis later labeled a 'crucible' – 'a transformative experience though which an individual comes to a new or an altered sense of identity'.

An adviser to four US presidents and perhaps the first modern leadership guru, Bennis was white-toothed, perma-tanned, California-based. He looked like a leader. Ironically perhaps, his actual experience of leading an organization aside from in wartime was disappointing. Bennis recounted a feeling of powerlessness as head of an academic institution. He looked out of his well-appointed leader's office and watched the gardener mowing the lawn and envied him his apparent independence and power. Undaunted, Bennis returned to the academic fray to make better sense of leadership.

His research explored how the crucible experience was instrumental in shaping leadership qualities. 'We found that something magical happens in the crucible – an alchemy whereby fear and suffering are transformed into something glorious and redemptive. This process reveals, if it does not create, leadership, the ability to inspire and move others to action.'

Whether fighting in a war, or overcoming a disaster, or some significant event in their life, good or bad, leaders are able to construct a narrative around it, about the challenge, how they dealt with it, learnt and became better leaders as a result.

Of course, all this begs the question, is it possible to create your own crucible? Vietnams of the mind. Most of us, thankfully, spend our lives outside war zones and prison walls.

Bennis believed it was possible to forge our own formative leadership experiences. 'I think they are created all the time,' he said:

> We all experience crucibles but what do we do at the back end of them? Do we learn from them? Do we extract wisdom from them? I have been puzzling about how do we create within our institutions the capacity to understand what goes on when organizations or individuals face crucibles. It isn't a question of how do we create them; they happen and happen almost all the time. Do we think of them as a dream so that when we wake up and brush our teeth it vaporizes or do we think about the dream and learn from that? It is the same thing about the crucibles. Having to fire people, being fired, being shipped to an office you don't like, thinking that you have been demoted when maybe you haven't. It's a matter of how organizations can use the crucibles of everyday life and extract wisdom from them to make organizations organically learn from the experiences they're undergoing. My concern is how do we use everyday crucibles which we're not sometimes conscious of.

The availability of crucibles was brought home to us talking with the CEO of Vodafone, Vittorio Colao. We asked how far his career was planned and the crucial events that had shaped it. 'A manager's career is so dependent on circumstances. I've never planned my life too much. I'm full of interests, personal and professional. I believe that life evolves and that you have to adjust. Career plan? No, I don't think that way,' said Colao:

> I always say when I speak to students that there have been three defining experiences in my life. One has been, believe it or not, the military – and, most importantly, military school. When I was in the mountain troops, I did things that I couldn't suspect I had the

energy for; and I realized that people have almost unlimited energy and unlimited possibilities. We just need to believe in the future.

The second key time in my life was at McKinsey, where I learned the power of honest, thorough, clinical analysis of facts, as opposed to words and perceptions. McKinsey believes in giving clients the truth even if they don't want to hear it. McKinsey's power of going below the surface, getting down to root causes, makes an impact. One of the things they always did at McKinsey, when faced with a new assignment, was – instead of analyzing the annual report and so forth – to talk to customers and suppliers of the client. They will always tell you so much more about the company than you could read in its annual report.

For Colao the third defining experience – his crucible – came with his experience at Vodafone Italy, which was then called Omnitel Pronto-Italia:

It was incredibly entrepreneurial and all about the power of creating something totally and in the right way. When people are asked to lead companies that have been in existence for a long time, they find that they have legacies to manage, which can be limiting. By contrast, at Vodafone Italy, I found how exciting it can be to join with others in that type of entrepreneurial environment, seeing people working and doing things that they would not believe that they could, just because of the enthusiasm of the vision and set up.

Talking to other leaders, similar crucibles were described. Interestingly, many leaders remember sales jobs early in their working lives. For example, Chris Rodrigues, then CEO of Visa, told a formative story about selling dog food from the back of a car in London.

Sir Peter Lampl, founder of the Sutton Trust, shared the starting points of his career: 'I read chemistry at Oxford, then I got a job at Beechams in marketing, which was a good thing to do because brand management was hot. I left Oxford, went on holiday and started working in September. I went straight on a sales training course with Beechams to sell pharmaceuticals. I did that for six weeks and then they put me out on the road as a salesman, selling to GPs [general practitioners] and hospital doctors. You're treated like a subhuman. But it was great experience.'

They may not have been going into war, but talking to these leaders it was clear these were the experiences which had made them into the leaders they now are; career crucibles out of which they emerged as leaders.

Resources

Warren Bennis' later intellectual flowering included *On Becoming A Leader* (Perseus Books, 1989) and (with Robert Thomas), 'Crucibles of leadership' (*Harvard Business Review*, September 2002).

Our interviews with Vittorio Colao and Sir Peter Lampl were published in *Business Strategy Review* (www.london.edu).

Leaders listen #16

'I hope we never lose sight of one fact ... that this was all started by a mouse,' Walt Disney was fond of saying in his later years. The origins of Disney's mousey inspiration are told in myriad variations. At one time it was reputed that in his early career he befriended a family of mice in his office. Their regular appearances on his drawing board proved inspirational. Nice story.

Alternatively, the *Daily Sketch* reported in 1938 that 'On his way back to Hollywood in an upper berth he could not sleep. The continuous but slight creaking of the woodwork in his compartment sounded like a million mice in conference. The idea made him laugh and in that split second Mickey Mouse was born'. Perhaps.

The facts are that the mouse in question began life as Mortimer Mouse. Walt Disney's wife, Lillian, did not take to the name and suggested Mickey as a replacement. Walt listened – whether this was to placate his wife or out of some deep realization that Mickey was the ideal name to launch a business empire will never be known. (Of course, why Mickey works and Mortimer doesn't is a matter of serious debate – 'Maybe Mickey Mouse didn't sound quite as onomatopoeic as Mortimer Mouse, but was a friendlier, more informal name, suggesting an affinity with the common man,' observed one book with due solemnity.)

On Sunday 18 November 1928, Mickey Mouse featured in one of the only cinematic epics of seven minutes in length: *Steamboat Willie*. This was the first cartoon which synchronized sound and action. *Steamboat*

Willie reversed the tide of Walt Disney's fortunes. Listening to Mrs. Disney was the turning point.

The role of listening in leadership is well established. And yet, it is commonly notable by its absence. You might have watched *Undercover Boss*, a popular TV series whose format has been sold throughout the world. The format is simple: a boss is disguised and sent to work at the front line of the organization. The results are predictable and predictably entertaining.

In a recent UK show, the CEO of a chain of nightclubs was dispatched to work at a selection of his clubs. He was surprised to find that young people drank themselves into a stupor or A&E (the emergency room). He was even more surprised to find that the toilets at the nightclubs weren't very pleasant at the end of a long evening. Along the way, as his eyes were opened to the reality of his business, the CEO met some of the exceptional people working for the company – uncomplaining cleaners, managers who do virtually everything, young marketers getting people through the doors.

Week after week in the show, leaders (or supposed leaders) encounter the reality of their businesses and are surprised. This begs an obvious question: why don't they know what goes on in their organization?

Perhaps it is a lack of curiosity. Perhaps they are trapped in some sort of corporate comfort zone. Perhaps it is a lack of imagination, a failure to link the decision to sell shots in a UK nightclub for less than a pound each with rampant drunkenness.

Whatever the reasons, it is inexcusable for leaders not to understand the day-to-day reality of their organization.

Indeed, the most impressive and successful leaders have an intimate understanding of the minutiae of their organization. They also know that any organization relies on people doing fantastic things and going beyond the call of duty.

Leaders need to be on the lookout for new trends, actively eliciting information from a range of stakeholders, including customers, partners and employees. Rosabeth Moss Kanter of Harvard Business School suggests cultivating a series of 'listening posts' to help with this. She calls this skill tuning in to the environment. Do not tune out to the bad news about the business, either.

Listening is required because leadership is about challenging prevailing wisdom in the organization. Leaders absorb information from different sources, look for the patterns in the information, and then construct new patterns, question assumptions, find a new lens through which to view problems. Job rotations, interdisciplinary projects and interactions outside the organization all help with kaleidoscopic thinking, as Kanter calls it.

Only listening and tuning in enables the leader to appreciate a timeless truth: my agenda is not your agenda. Ever.

'One of the things that I have learned is that everybody who walks through my door in my office has a bias. They are biased in some way and sometimes they don't even know that they are biased,' Novartis CEO Joe Jimenez told us. 'The key to this job is to determine what is that bias and what should I really learn from the conversation that I just had with that person. It becomes a very interesting internal discussion that I have with myself as I am having meetings with people: to really identify their bias and search for the truth that is being communicated because the truth is in there somewhere.'

You have to go looking for the truth. Before interviewing Vittorio Colao, CEO of Vodafone, we were in a Vodafone store and asked the sales assistant whether she knew anything about him. 'Oh yes, he comes in quite a lot,' she replied – Vodafone is a big company, but the CEO makes the time to visit stores. 'One of the problems for CEOs is that we risk living in a bubble: only taking British Airways, living in airport lounges and corporate boardrooms and talking only to other CEOs. My challenge is to keep learning new things in both my personal life and my business life,' Colao told us.

At an airport early in the morning Colao noticed that one of Vodafone's airport shops was closed at 6.15 a.m. and next door there were three shops open. Of such observations is leadership made.

Similarly, we talked with Ben Lewis, the CEO of the River Island retail chain. He had worked in the stores so knew how they worked. He reckoned that he could assess a store's performance and problems in a forty-five-minute visit. This was something he did routinely every week. When we spoke it was a Wednesday and he had already paid a visit to the Brent Cross store in London and was heading over to White City later in the afternoon. He had managed to take in three stores in one day during the previous week.

'I have to be able to look at product, walk into a shop and have a sense and a knowledge about whether it's right or wrong and how to fix it,' he says. Then there is the trawling of retail sites to see alternative approaches, Facebook posts, online blogs, student chat rooms and more. 'I am hungry for information all the time. I review customer service comments, I talk to store managers, I talk to friends and the children of friends, I talk to staff that work in the fitting room, I talk to the buying team about the information they're gathering.'

These leaders are grounded. They understand how their business works and the issues facing the people who work for them on the front line. They look, listen and learn.

But it is not only in retail businesses where this connectedness with reality is important. We asked a director of the Japanese company Fujitsu what he remembered about his first day with the company. It was over thirty years ago so it was a feat of memory. He paused and thought. 'Yes, I remember. I was sent to work in a bank, a Fujitsu customer. It was unclear who worked for the bank and who worked for Fujitsu. That has always stuck with me – we work closely with our customers because we need to understand their needs and businesses.'

None of this is rocket science. Leadership isn't. But, leading an organization, any organization, requires attention to detail and a connection to the reality of how the it works for customers, users and employees. There is no short cut. Listen up.

Resources

Stuart's interview with Vittorio Colao was published as 'Total communicator' in *Business Strategy Review*, Autumn 2010.

Deans of leadership   #17

We were at the business school INSEAD recently at a launch event and symposium for a book we had published. Towards the end of the day INSEAD's dean Ilian Mihov popped in. He made an informed comment about the subject under discussion, referenced his own research, thanked us all for being there, made a self-deprecating joke and left. We followed up with an email to him. He replied quickly and helpfully. This is active rather than passive leadership.

Earlier in the same week we had been at Europe's tallest building, the Shard in London. Warwick Business School was opening its London operation in the building. Boris Johnson, the Mayor of London, performed the official opening. As we were enjoying a pre-event coffee beside the Shard, we saw the mayor make his own entrance. He did not arrive in some mayoral limousine surrounded by flunkeys and bodyguards. No, he arrived on a bicycle in a crumpled suit. As he dismounted his bike and took off his helmet to reveal his trademark hair, it was clear that everyone noticed him.

So what did Boris Johnson tell the assembled dignitaries and well wishers? The mayor's speech at the opening ceremony was entirely in character. He sang the praises of London and cited a welter of statistics suggesting that the world's greatest city was indeed just that. To this he added some relevant references to Warwick and Shakespeare.

The dean of WBS, Mark Taylor, is another active leader. Setting up shop in London's most iconic new building was a clear signal of intent. WBS could have taken up less lofty (and less expensive) lodgings in another part of the capital. But Taylor has no intention of letting the business school be overlooked, literally or figuratively. After years in the parochial wings, Warwick is moving to center stage.

None of what Ilian Mihov, Mark Taylor or Boris Johnson did was rocket science. Mihov displayed knowledge of the subject, Taylor clearly sees WBS as a force to be reckoned with and Johnson knows his Shakespeare. But what they displayed is the essence of leadership.

Being there

The mundane secret of leadership is that turning up is hugely important. Ilian Mihov is based in Singapore and when we encountered him he was at INSEAD in Fontainebleau, France. He had back-to-back meetings all day and was popping in and out of those meetings to greet and connect with people. He realized that a few minutes with him in the room is important, a handshake still beats an email.

Taylor, too, understands that if you want to be a player in the financial center of London, you can't do it from a campus in the Midlands. You have to be there.

Being seen

For the leader, high visibility is essential. We worked with one organization whose leader was nicknamed the invisible man because he was there so infrequently and, when he was, stayed in his office. Boris Johnson is highly visible. You may not agree with his transport policies but if you have seen him cycling in London you know that he must have some understanding of the issues faced by Londoners.

Beating being boring

Leaders say the same thing again and again. Leadership is boring. Boris Johnson has recited his stats about how multicultural London is thousands of times. That is his job. Leaders deliver the same messages time and time again, but they do so with energy and enthusiasm at all times.

Being civil

Leadership is still sadly seen in macho, alpha male terms. Actually, the most persuasive leaders we have encountered are courteous and polite. They reply to emails, they say thank you, they are inclusive in discussions, they are respectful and curious.

Being a leader

There is no template for leaders. They come in all shapes and sizes. But what is notable about the most successful leaders is that they have a strong desire to make things happen. They want to help their organizations move forward, guiding them in the right direction.

When we first met him several years ago, Mark Taylor explained that if an organization or institution is not moving forward then it is falling behind. Contrast this with passive leaders, serving out their time, content to try to maintain the status quo. That is not leadership. That is being a bystander, not a leader.

The best leaders want to lead. They radiate leadership, there is a kind of force field of leadership, which surrounds – and perhaps protects – them. For them it is not enough to simply stand by and watch. They embody leadership. They live it.

Aiming blind and big   #18

In 1907, Henry Ford professed that his aim was to 'build a motor car for the great multitude ... It will be so low in price that no man making a good salary will be unable to own one – and enjoy with his family the blessing of hours of pleasure in God's great open spaces ... everybody will be able to afford one, and everyone will have one. The horse will have disappeared from our highways, the automobile will be taken for granted'. Ford's commitment to lowering prices cannot be doubted. Between 1908 and 1916 he reduced prices by 58 percent – at a time when demand was such that he could easily have raised prices. What drove him to do so? The drive to achieve his vision.

'Posterity will not excuse you if you did not dream big,' says Narayana Murthy, one of the founders of Infosys. 'You owe it to your customers, your colleagues, your investors, and society. Every major civilization, every great advance in science and technology, and every great company is built on a big dream.'

Big dreams are not the sole preserve of large organizations. While leading large organizations, whether they be hospitals, companies, even nations, is clearly demanding, leadership is also practiced in much smaller contexts – in families, in teams, in small entrepreneurial start-ups. Indeed, some of the most inspirational examples come from leaders in such organizations who have big dreams and compelling visions of what they would like to achieve.

Talking to entrepreneurial leaders you never know what to expect. Sometimes their business idea appears hardly developed. Other times it is so highly developed that they can appear to be caught in an entrepreneurial straightjacket of great intentions. Likewise, the personalities and characters of the entrepreneurs vary wildly. Some MBA types seem fixated on spreadsheets and preparing for every known and unknown variable. Others appear more pragmatic, willing to go with the flow.

Pragmatism should not be interpreted as a sign of weakness. This was brought home to us talking with Sarah Wood of Unruly, a marketing company that started life in 2006. There was, she laughingly admitted, no master plan. Indeed, there was no plan.

'The idea didn't come first. The idea of Unruly came after we'd founded the company,' she says. This, we observe, is not the conventional approach. Most companies have an idea of what they want to do but no idea of how to make it a commercial reality. 'I don't think there is a right way or a wrong way. Hopefully we're proof of that.'

Wood joined forces with Scott Button, whom she had known since university, and Matt Cooke. Button and Cooke had worked together at Connextra and used some of their profits from their stakes in Connextra as seed funding for the new business. The trio reckoned they had enough money for eighteen months – 'A runway big enough to have lots of ideas, but short enough that we needed those ideas to get traction and if they didn't work we needed to move onto the next one'.

Though Wood describes herself as an 'accidental entrepreneur' there is nothing accidental about her or the company's ambitions. The trio of Unruly founders may not have had a killer idea but they had something that can be even more powerful: bold ambition.

We did have an end game and it was to build a billion-dollar business and we were very clear about that right from the start, and we still are. We want to build a billion-dollar business. That's still what we're shooting for and that really helps us make decisions because when we're looking for new products and we're making decisions about who we acquire, we say to ourselves, is this helping us get to be a billion-dollar business?

This is not only great entrepreneurial shorthand; it also works for leaders. The best leaders have a killer question they use to test decisions against. What is your shorthand for success?

This is not decorative. A thrilling, exciting purpose is vital to creating a positive culture. It is the job of leaders to create excitement. They are Chief Excitement Officers. This is how Warren Bennis put it: 'The new leader keeps reminding people of what's important. Organizations drift into entropy and the bureaucratization of imagination when they forget what's important. Simple to say, but that one sentence is one of the few pieces of advice I suggest to leaders: remind your people of what's important. A powerful enough vision can transform what would otherwise be routine and drudgery into collectively focused energy.'

Leaders provide purpose by describing the big picture, the story of the future and the role of each and every individual in making it reality. They constantly remind people of what really matters.

The undefinable nature of leadership and its relentless focus on the insecure world of change is disquieting, daunting and, perhaps, misses one of the big positive messages of leadership: it should be intent on building something. Leaders are builders – but not of monuments to their own brilliance. They want to achieve a goal, to create something which lasts.

Ask yourself another simple question: what am I building?

One person we have encountered who made the leader-as-builder link is Jimmy Maymann, the Danish CEO of the *Huffington Post*. 'I like to build things; companies, houses, sand castles, you name it,' he says. His building project of the moment is to take the online newspaper global. 'At this point it is about making a difference, doing something that will change or disrupt something. It's really not about the money, it's about that challenge,' he explains. 'For me, that is what's important, that's what's getting me up in the morning. The only thing I want to do is build great things, and I would like to be the one that helps HuffPost to become a global media brand.'

Warren Bennis liked to tell the story of the Manhattan Project. 'The US Army had recruited talented engineers from all over the United

States for special duty on the project. They were assigned to work on the primitive computers of the period [1943–45], doing energy calculations and other tedious jobs,' he told us:

> But the Army, obsessed with security, refused to tell them anything specific about the project. They didn't know that they were building a weapon that could end the war or even what their calculations meant. They were simply expected to do the work, which they did slowly and not very well. Richard Feynman, who supervised the technicians, prevailed on his superiors to tell the recruits what they were doing and why. Permission was granted to lift the veil of secrecy, and Robert Oppenheimer gave them a special lecture on the nature of the project and their own contribution.

The rest is history, but it is only by aiming bold and big that history can begin to be made.

Resources

For more information on Sarah Wood and Unruly see 'Unruly rules', *Business Strategy Review* (Winter, 2014). As we went to press, it was announced that the company had been acquired by News Corp. Bold and big indeed.

Leaders wear cardigans

#19

The world's biggest supercomputer is a big deal. A few years ago we talked to members of the Japanese team involved in developing a computer nicknamed K. The name was a play on the Japanese word 'kei' for the number 10 to the power of 16. It is a big number and it was a big build with a $1 billion development budget and over 1,000 people involved. Development began in 2007 and ended in 2012 with the K being celebrated as the fastest of the fastest.

We met the managers and leaders from the Japanese company Fujitsu involved in this huge project. It was striking how down to earth they were. The Fujitsu team were not classic Silicon Valley material. They were neither hip nor cool. There were no jeans, not even chinos. No casual wear; nothing casual at all. Indeed, when we met the project manager he looked like a typical middle-aged Japanese corporate man, wearing a suit with a cardigan to stave off the Tokyo winter chill. Ordinary people involved in an extraordinary project.

We also talked to Aiichirou Inque, a gentle, affable yet intense man. After twenty-seven years with the company we could have forgiven him for an air of ennui. Instead, when we spoke he was a ball of creative energy, excited and under pressure in equal measure. 'At my previous company I couldn't do the things I wanted to do. I wanted to build something by myself, not just to use it, but to build it. For me that's what it is all about.'

And now Inque was charged with developing the K Computer then being built at Japan's Institute of Physical and Chemical Research, known as Riken, near Osaka.

The term supercomputer was coined in the 1960s to describe a computer that is at the frontier of current computing capability. Today, supercomputers are capable of quickly performing large-scale and advanced calculations that are difficult or impossible to solve with conventional computers. For example, they are used in quantum physics, weather forecasting and climate research. Supercomputers are used instead of experimentation for physical simulations such as testing airplanes in wind tunnels and research into nuclear fusion. They are also used to compute the structures and properties of chemical compounds, biological macromolecules, polymers and crystals.

The Batista heart operation is one example of the new supercomputer's life-changing potential. The Batista operation is an experimental open-heart surgery procedure that aims to reverse the effects of remodeling in cases of end-stage dilated cardiomyopathy. Invented in 1994 by Brazilian surgeon Randas Batista, the operation involves removing a portion of viable tissue from the left ventricle to reduce its size.

Although several studies showed benefits from this procedure, studies at the Cleveland Clinic concluded that it was associated with a high failure rate. One use of the K computer that Fujitsu is exploring is the development of a heart simulator which would allow surgeons to anticipate the likely effects of the Batista procedure – to determine whether it would be beneficial to a patient and assess the likelihood of complications.

But this is only possible if Fujitsu's engineers work closely with the doctors who are highly skilled in performing the operation. 'The point where the computer engineer talks to the doctor is key,' says Inque. 'That ability to work with customers and end users is part of Fujitsu's DNA.' Innovation and leadership often require collaboration and listening in equal measure.

The potential benefits for mankind are huge. But so are the challenges of building the world's most powerful computer, as Inque acknowledges. 'The reality is that because the supercomputer is so large we will and are encountering things we haven't experienced before or don't really expect. That's part of the challenge – and it's also part of the excitement. We are really pushing the boundaries of what is possible with computing.'

Such a project is also highly inspirational for Fujitsu employees.

'I want the young engineers working on this project to be excited and to enjoy their work,' says Aiichirou Inque. 'But let's be clear: the K Computer will make the future for Fujitsu, Japan and for human beings. It will give us the ability to look at the weather of the future and there are a huge number of healthcare uses. That's what I mean about its power to change humanity. A computer is just a big box; what's interesting is to see it as a tool to help mankind and society.'

The current market for supercomputers is estimated to be around $9 billion and Fujitsu hopes to control 10 percent of that market by tapping into growing demand in Europe, especially in Germany, France and the UK. What makes this all the more exciting is the advent of Big Data. Collecting and making sense of large amounts of data requires big computing power. Big Data and supercomputers could be a marriage made in heaven.

'We are already working with customers so we understand their needs and those of the eventual end users,' Inque told us. 'With something like a supercomputer it is often very difficult for the customers to know how to make use of the product. We have to get out and talk to them to better understand what they are doing every day and how the computer can play a role. In the end, first and foremost, the computer needs to work and, second, it needs to be heavily used. That's how its success should be judged. Does it make a difference to human life?'

In all our conversations with the supercomputer team at Fujitsu the word leadership was never used. The greater purpose of the project was constantly emphasized. The purpose provided leadership and the job of the project leaders was simply and repeatedly to communicate that purpose for it is the creation and communication of purpose which lies at the heart of leadership.

Resources

The inside story of Fujitsu is told by Kyoko Katase and Atsushi Tajima in *Fortune Favors the Brave* (Nikkei, 2012).

Leaders begin with the future

There is a stereotype of the CEO as thinker. The CEO withdraws into strategic seclusion and emerges with a compelling vision of the future and how to get there. The exemplar of this was Bill Gates who disappeared for 'think weeks' to consider Microsoft's future. He reportedly sat in a cabin, and read and thought through trends, challenges and opportunities. It worked.

While not every leader has Bill Gates' appetite for monastic seclusion and contemplation, a focus on the future is important. 'The most successful leader of all is one who sees another picture not yet actualized,' observed Mary Parker Follett over a century ago.

As Henry Mintzberg's research shows, the present has a nasty habit of overwhelming contemplation of the future. In their work Gary Hamel and C. K. Prahalad lamented that senior executives devote less than 3 percent of their energy to 'building a corporate perspective of the future'.

Work by London Business School's Rajesh Chandy (along with Jaideep Prabhu and Manjot Yadav) used data from American retail banking to look at the link between CEOs and innovation. The research concludes: 'CEOs who attend to the future are faster at developing new technological opportunities and faster at developing initial products based on these technologies, and better at deploying these initial products.' If you know where you are going, you might get there quicker.

For leaders, the past is history. Time and time again, we are struck by the ability of leaders to exist in the moment, to focus on the now and what they want to achieve rather than being imprisoned by the past. They are energetically present.

Take Vivek Singh, chef and CEO of the Cinnamon Club restaurant group. The need to keep pushing himself and his team forward is what Singh admits keeps him awake at night. 'At the back of my mind is how do I make sure that even very good people, who have grown a lot, are challenged and engaged and aspire to the next level. It's not good enough to think I've done a very good job and that's enough. You have got to go forward and want to do other things. But, what are those other things, and what could those things be?'

There is a restless energy to Vivek Singh. The next challenge can't come quickly enough. Anyone who spends hours in steaming kitchens tends to need energy to burn. He is a restless improver and tinkerer. Dishes are chopped and changed, never revived. 'If you leave something on the menu too long, people get comfortable with it. And once they get comfortable with it, and start recognizing it, they won't try other things and experiment,' says Singh. 'For us it's so important we change; change is the thing that is a constant on our menus. No matter how successful you are, you always become a victim of your own success; therefore, we need to accommodate change.'

Indeed, the most popular dishes are clinically eliminated. At the end of every year the most successful dish is taken off the menu and re-placed. The change, he explains, ensures that comfort zones never become permanent. 'The dishes that sell the most can be overrated, in the sense they might account for 40 percent of sales. So, at the Cinnamon Club that would mean 40,000 people are having one dish. After a while, no matter how passionate they are, fatigue will set in for the chef so that the excitement, love and passion clearly aren't there.'

Change keeps the chefs fresh. At the other end, Singh is equally counter-intuitive and loath to change dishes simply because they aren't selling. 'If it doesn't sell, it says something about the people who are coming in, or it says something about the people who are selling it. So if it doesn't sell at all, it means either my staff aren't able to explain the dish, or people aren't adventurous enough.'

This is a confident assertion, assuming that the food itself is good. Vivek Singh nods. He gives the example of bheja fry, which is on the menu at Cinnamon Soho and which is one of the most popular dishes in India: lambs brains. The Cinnamon take on the recipe is very different and was entered by Singh into a restaurant critics' competition. 'People said "chef, are you sure?". But we won a prize. It pushes barriers, redefines expectations. In the restaurant we serve six hundred to seven hundred people a week, and might sell ten. It may not sell, but it makes a statement about what we believe in, what we are doing, how we are different. It immediately sets us apart from anything else that anybody else is doing.'

Vivek Singh's energetic embrace of the future was echoed when we met with Steve Radcliffe, a leadership and development consultant who has worked alongside a number of CEOs of major organizations, from Unilever to the UK's Civil Service. He is the author of *Leadership Plain and Simple*. Radcliffe is an intense and energetic Lancastrian with a flair for polite bluntness. His avowed mission is to persuade people that leadership does not have to be difficult. Most people can learn to be a more effective leader, whether they are the CEO of a multinational corporation or have just started work.

'It absolutely doesn't matter where you are in an organization. You can be in your first job, you can have no direct reports,' he says. 'You can have a team or run a department. You can head an organization. And you can work in a school, charity or global business. It really doesn't matter because I've seen inspiring leadership from people in all these positions and I've realized that the fundamentals of leadership are the same for any situation.'

Whatever the position, there are three essential ingredients to focus on, says Radcliffe: Future – Engage – Deliver.

Leading has to start with the future and where leaders want to get to. Only by having a strong sense of where they need to be in the future will they be able to persuade others to commit to that future too. The more passionately leaders care about that future, the greater the positive impact on their followers.

Next, leaders have to engage, says Radcliffe. As he points out this is not 'communicating to' or 'presenting at' or 'telling'. This is engaging people both in the vision of the future and with the leader. The qualities required to achieve this include 'integrity, openness and consistency', Radcliffe notes. Finally a leader needs to deliver or, more to the point, help the team to help the leader deliver.

Improving in these areas means building and flexing leadership muscles. We have all got them; it is just a question of exercising them, effectively. The future is here.

Resources

Steve Radcliffe, *Leadership Plain and Simple* (FT Prentice Hall, 2010).

Olympic leadership

We worked a while ago on a book about the business turnaround of the Olympic Games. It prompted us to look into the evolution of the modern Olympic movement and to pay a visit to the Olympic Museum in Lausanne.

In the late nineteenth century things moved at a more sedentary pace. As a result, the story behind the creation of the modern Olympic Games has a lengthy period of gestation. It was in 1889 that the first important decision in a trail of decisions was made when the French government commissioned Pierre de Coubertin to report on the nation's physical fitness and methods used to promote what it called 'physical culture'.

De Coubertin took three years. He traveled widely and examined how other countries nurtured physical fitness among their people. 'Everywhere I met discord and civil war had been established between the advocates of this or that form of exercise; this state of affairs seemed to me to be the result of an excessive specialization,' he said. 'The gymnasts showed bad will towards the rowers, the fencers towards the cyclists, the rifle marksmen towards the lawn-tennis players; peace did not even reign among the adepts of the same sports; the supporters of German gymnastics denied all merit to the Swedish and the rules of American football seemed to the English players not to make common sense.' Eventually he returned to present his findings at the Sorbonne on 25 November 1892. In his lecture, de Coubertin recommended that international sports competitions be held periodically. The germ of an idea was planted. It was then left.

It reached the next stage in its life when de Coubertin convened an international conference in Paris. Here, he suggested that a modern version of Ancient Greece's Olympic Games be created. It was decided that the event be held every four years. The conference attracted attendees from twelve countries and twenty-one other nations expressed an interest. A groundswell was emerging.

The conference led to the creation of the International Olympic Committee with de Coubertin as General Secretary. In laying down the rules of the modern Olympics, the Committee made a number of important decisions. They decided that participants would compete regardless of race, color, creed, class or politics and that there would be no financial prizes. 'Olympism is not a system, it is a state of mind that can permeate a wide variety of modes of expression and no single race or era can claim a monopoly of it,' said de Coubertin.

In 1896 the first modern Olympic Games were held in Athens – the ancient city had offered to be a permanent home for the Games, but the Committee, and de Coubertin particularly, advocated that the Olympic Games be hosted by a different nation on each occasion. Forty thousand people came to watch the opening ceremony on 6 April 1896. De Coubertin expressed his hope that 'my idea will unite all in an athletic brotherhood, in a peaceful event whose impact will, I hope be of great significance'.

What does this story offer for the modern leader? First, state your values upfront. The Olympic ideal is based on simple values and precepts which were stated at the very start of the movement. They have lasted.

De Coubertin moved from having a vision to reality. Visions can become reality. Really.

And then there is his Olympian persistence. Pierre de Coubertin's heart is buried at Olympia. His epitaph reads: 'The main issue in life is not the victory but the fight. The essential is not to have won but to have fought well.' The genesis of the Olympic Games was slow, but de Coubertin stuck with his vision, which continues to thrive.

Resources

The business side of the Olympic Games is excellently told in the book we mentioned, *Olympic Turnaround* by Michael Payne (Infinite Ideas, 2012).

The leader repeats   #22

In political campaigns, would-be leaders have their stump speeches. These are the inspirational comfort blankets they produce when they are wheeled out in front of yet another audience. Business leaders have much the same thing. CEOs have neat five-minute spiels they produce on demand for employees, investors, the media and analysts.

Look, for example, at the press cuttings of well-known CEOs. You can guarantee that the same stories, strategies and statistics are religiously recounted. Repetition is safe territory.

But no leader can pay lip service to repetition. Indeed, the biggest sin a leader can commit is to go through the motions, to appear bored by repeating the same corporate goal for the nth time.

This was brought home to us talking with the CEO of Vodafone, Vittorio Colao. A thoughtful man, Colao had a very clear idea of his role and where he added value to the company. It was notable, as he spoke, that as he described it, his role was almost humdrum. There was no gung-ho leadership here, just someone acting as a highly attuned and intelligent conduit to release the talent and power in the organization; quietly impressive. Colao says:

> My role in providing the glue is really based on three key elements. I start from the value set, because the value set is more important than anything else. It is the Vodafone way of doing things, a way of respecting the customers, a way of positioning our brand. It's something that we would never compromise on, and that's the most important thing that keeps everything together.

The second is the sharing of the experience, the values, the competencies and the solutions. I was in Turkey recently, and I discovered a fantastic solution for handling calls in the call centers, which I've never heard before; and I said, "This is great". Spreading that idea throughout the company is part of my job, and this is a way of adding glue to a big enterprise.

The third thing, quite frankly, is that my role is to go around and explain the future and how Vodafone must find the right local path into its evolution. The evolution from voice to data (and from mobile-only to total communications) is going to take place everywhere in the world. Whether it's Ghana, Tanzania or Germany, our transition is going to happen everywhere; but each part of Vodafone must find the best way to make the transition happen locally.

The timing will be different and the way it will happen will be different; but, if I have given each locale the framework and made sure that every market then finds its own path, a really good thing will have happened: each part of the company will have a greater sense of ownership and a greater sense of belonging. I present the vision of the future, then help each locale to find the best path and the best way to reach it.

Traveling the world hammering home the same messages time and time again is what leaders do. It is the job. One of the most striking things about leadership is that it is often boring, repetitive work. The audiences might be larger, the stakes higher, but a great deal of repetition comes with the job. Leaders like Vittorio Colao are endlessly communicating much the same messages, the three elements he has decided are fundamental for the company's future.

And you have to deliver these messages with energy and commitment every single time. 'If you're the CEO of a multi-billion-dollar corporation, everyone in that room is looking at your face. They're listening to every word you say and it matters to them,' says the executive coach Marshall Goldsmith. 'Now CEOs are humans. Sometimes you're in a meeting, they're making presentations, it's boring, you already know what they're going to say, you've got to go to the bathroom. It doesn't matter. They're all looking at your face, and if you don't look interested and caring and motivated, you demoralize people. That's what being a professional is.'

There is another issue here: consistency. Leaders cannot say one thing to one audience and quote another thing to the next group they encounter. This seems obvious, but we have seen leaders do just that on many occasions.

Inconsistency undermines at every level. Says INSEAD's Gianpiero Petriglieri: 'We know in history that people forgive leaders for murder but they don't forgive them for inconsistency. The classic disappointment with charismatic leaders is that they articulate their vision so beautifully and they embody it with such great purity that people think some profound transformation is going to happen. Then the realization inevitably meets constraints and what happens is people blame the leader.'

For the leader, the ideal mix appears to be an ability to deliver the same messages repeatedly and consistently, but with the passion and excitement essential to rally people to the organizational cause. It is a demanding leadership recipe.

It takes two   #23

Do we have unrealistic expectations of our corporate and political leaders? This was one of the questions we asked Harvard Business School's Rosabeth Moss Kanter when we spoke. Her answer was illuminating: 'Yes. If the expectation is that a single leader can do it all then it is unrealistic. But it is also interesting how much a single leader can set in motion. In turnarounds it is quite striking how much fresh leadership can accomplish by unlocking talent and potential that was already there in the organization but which was stifled by rules, regulations and bureaucracy.'

So, individual leaders can be hugely influential and powerful. They can change things. But, and it is an awfully big but, leaders are nothing without followers. And some follow more closely than others. Look around at many great leaders and you will see a reliable accomplice at their side – think Charlie Munger and Warren Buffett, William Whitelaw and Margaret Thatcher, Alistair Campbell and Tony Blair and so on. Leadership is often a duet rather than a solo.

So, the John Wayne type of heroic leadership loner is history? We asked leadership guru Warren Bennis. 'Yes, the Lone Ranger is dead,' he replied:

Instead of the individual problem solver we have a new model for creative achievement. People like Steve Jobs or Walt Disney headed groups and found their own greatness in them. The new leader is a pragmatic dreamer, a person with an original but attainable vision. Ironically, the leader is able to realize his or her dream only if the others are free to do exceptional work. Typically, the leader is the one who recruits the others, by making the vision so palpable and seductive that they see it, too, and eagerly sign up.

Chris Gibson-Smith, chairman of the London Stock Exchange and a former BP executive, emphasized the teamwork element of business – and of leadership: 'Business is a team-based enterprise; there are almost no exceptions. The combined brain is a bigger brain than the individual brain. There is almost no problem that is not better solved by engaging a group of the right sort of people with the right skills in the solution harmoniously.'

Richard Hytner, deputy chairman of Saatchi & Saatchi, has studied leadership duos and champions the role of the much neglected number two. The reality, he points out, is that we can't all be number ones – there aren't enough number one roles in the first place and many of us would be ill-suited to them anyway. 'The truth is we spend most of our careers, even as heads of functions, factories, geographies or service lines, serving at least one master, yet choose to shape our identity as early as we can as a number one, a supreme leader. Where, after all, is the glamour in shaping an identity as one who merely advises or assists?' says Hytner.

What is needed is a new model of leadership for all leading players, one that assigns roles clearly and aspirationally, and one that encourages more people to discover, through choice, not just the well-trodden path to the top but the joys of leading from the shadows as a destination in its own right. By conflating all types of leader into just two: A – the ultimately Accountable – and C – the Consiglieri (there are usually more than one) who liberate, enlighten and deliver for the A, the role of the second is elevated to equal amongst firsts, circumventing the tyranny of the number one's titular supremacy and the prevailing undercurrent of 'second syndrome'.

The original consiglieri were the advisers to leaders of Italian mafia families, made famous by Mario Puzo's novel, *The Godfather*. As Richard Hytner makes clear, consiglieri also operate in more legitimate fields.

They are the deputies, assistants and counselors who support, inform and advise the final decision-makers of organizations. Consiglieri – or Cs – are leader makers and leaders in their own right. While only a few go on to become ultimate A leaders, many more perform roles in which they make, shape, illuminate and enhance the success of the out-and-out A leader and the organization.

'The majority of consiglieri positively embrace their roles,' says Hytner:

They have not settled gloomily for C after having their love for A spurned. They have learnt the joys of influencing As whom they admire and respect. They wish to be close to power across their organizations and to have autonomy to get their jobs done. They are insatiable learners, accruing new experience as if their life depends on it (which, as some consiglieri have discovered, it sometimes does). They have found their greatest and most consistent pleasure in helping others reach their full potential.

The first question for leaders is whether they are prepared to recognize that leadership is not an activity performed by them in splendid isolation. The second is how they can best create and work with their own consiglieri.

Resources

Richard Hytner, *Consiglieri* (Profile, 2014).

Leaders know what matters   #24

'Attention is the chief bottleneck in organizational activity, and the bottleneck becomes narrower and narrower as we move to the top of organizations,' noted Herbert Simon.

Leaders establish what the organization needs to be paying attention to. They communicate the things that really matter – or the things they think really matter – in a personal and inspirational way. Without this level of focus, any leadership role can quickly become overwhelming.

'The communications and actions of CEOs reflect their attentional focus and help drive the culture and activities of the firm. Indeed a key strategic role of the CEO is to focus the attention of employees across alternative operations eventually driving them toward activities that are vital for the survival and growth of the firm,' says London Business School's Rajesh Chandy.

Modern organizations are large and complex. A CEO might have hundreds of thousands of employees looking to him or her for guidance, inspiration, direction and much more. Their days are packed with meeting after meeting, decision after decision, journey after journey.

What is amazing is how many survive and how they retain their focus on what matters to themselves and their organization. The best leaders know what matters and apply it to everything they do.

'The job of CEO has changed over the time that I've been CEO,' Tim Brown, CEO of the design company IDEO told us:

I have a set of four things in my mind, and the amount of time I spend on each of them varies across months and years. One of them is just making sure that the thing is ticking over, and we're not doing anything stupid. That's the least important of them. The next is a connecting to the organization, mostly for me to learn, but then also to connect. The third one is getting the IDEO message out into the world, and what we care about, what I care about personally. And then the fourth one is thinking about the future, where are we going.

There is nothing complicated in this. Tim Brown also told us that every year he tried to write down what he was going to hold himself accountable for and what he expected some other people to hold him accountable for.

Similarly, the CEO of GE, Jeff Immelt, talks of taking time out every weekend to review his previous week and his agenda for the forthcoming week. It is a simple process of taking stock.

Holding yourself to account is important. David Pyott, former CEO of Allergan (which brought the world Botox) also talked about the importance of setting an agenda:

In a lot of management (and particularly at the top), people don't step back often enough and ask, 'What is the agenda?' versus 'What is the agenda that other people have made for you?' You can become a slave of the organization. All the time I'm trying to say, what are the key things – probably five things – that we must get done? I'm very keen on making the appropriate agenda and being willing to change it.

Pyott talked about his early days as CEO:

When I came to Allergan, after about three weeks I wrote down on a piece of paper what I thought were the five most important things that I had to do. Then I put it in a drawer and didn't take it out again until four or five months later. Of the five things I'd written down, four of them were right and one was completely off beam. That was quite refreshing. It was a matter of checking it out before you go and drive a truck over the edge of the cliff.

Such lists are a performance shorthand. Some take this a little further. Every evening the executive coach Marshall Goldsmith receives a call from a friend asking the same questions. Some are about looking after himself and his health. Others are about looking after others. All are important.

There is, of course, the temptation to assume that such lists are trite and superficial. They may well be, but they are also very simple and memorable tools to help you identify what you value, what is important and how your daily activities are helping towards a clearly stated objective.

Investing in leadership #25

Headquartered in Omaha, Nebraska, Berkshire Hathaway *is* Warren Buffett. The two are inextricably linked – in corporate fact and stock-market mythology. The reality is that Berkshire Hathaway is no longer a humble textile company but a corporate entity, a shell inhabited by 316,000 employees and made real by the passage of dollars to and fro – but a shell with revenues of $194 billion.

In 1964 a share in Berkshire Hathaway Inc. was worth $19.46. They have now passed $200,000. These impressive figures have been much quoted as Buffett's success has been examined from every angle. Yet, if emulation is a measure of understanding, it appears little understood.

Above the maelstrom of analysts, commentators and private investors, stands Warren Buffett, a man of resolutely simple tastes, someone who oozes old-fashioned decency from every pore. As he has become more famous and Berkshire Hathaway ever more successful, Buffett's public utterances and writings have become more playful. 'As happens in Wall Street all too often, what the wise do in the beginning, fools do in the end,' he wrote in 1989. This was followed in 1990 by: 'Lethargy bordering on sloth remains the cornerstone of our investment style.' He has cornered many a market, but the one in homespun wisdom may be his surprising legacy.

Buffett advocates 'focused investing'. When gauging the wisdom of an investment, investors should look at five features: 'The certainty with which the long-term economic characteristics of the business can be evaluated; the certainty with which management can be evaluated, both as to its ability to realize the full potential of the business and to wisely employ its cash flows; the certainty with which management can be counted on to channel the reward from the business to the shareholders rather than to itself; the purchase price of the business; the levels of taxation and inflation that will be experienced and that will determine the degree by which an investor's purchasing-power return is reduced from his gross return.'

Buffett admits that many will find such criteria 'unbearably fuzzy'. This is only partly the case. Analysis can lead to conclusions about the long-term economic prospects of a business. Analysis can also establish what is a reasonable purchase price and help predict future macroeconomic conditions likely to impact on the investment. Where analysis falls down and things begin to become fuzzy is in assessing the incumbent management.

Buffett believes that executives should think and behave as owners of their businesses. He is critical, therefore, of the 'indiscriminate use' of stock options for senior executives. 'Managers actually apply a double standard to options,' Buffett writes. 'Nowhere in the business world are ten-year, fixed-price options on all or a portion of a business granted to outsiders. Ten months, in fact, would be regarded as extreme.' Such long-term options, argues Buffett, 'ignore the fact that retained earnings automatically build value and, second, ignore the carrying cost of capital'.

Buffett is a ponderous minimalist in an age of hyperactive behemoths. 'Charlie and I decided long ago that in an investment lifetime it's too hard to make hundreds of smart decisions ... Indeed, we'll now settle for one good idea a year. (Charlie says it's my turn.),' he wrote in 1993. Buffet is humorously embarrassed by the purchase of a corporate jet – 'It will not be long before Berkshire's entire net worth is consumed by its jet'.

Perhaps the single most important aspect of Buffett's leadership style is that 99 percent of his and his wife's net worth is in the company's shares. 'We want to make money only when our partners do and in exactly the same proportion,' he explains to shareholders. 'Moreover, when

I do something dumb, I want you to be able to derive some solace from the fact that my financial suffering is proportional to yours.' The investment secret of Warren Buffett is revealed: put all your eggs in one basket.

Time and time again, Buffett returns to the issue of sound management. He lauds some of his own managers: 'They love their businesses, they think like owners, and they exude integrity and ability.' This is the quintessence of Buffett's philosophy. Given the right conditions, good managers produce good companies. Never invest in badly managed companies. 'Charlie Munger, our vice chairman, and I really have only two jobs,' says Buffett. 'One is to attract and keep outstanding managers to run our various operations'. The other is capital allocation.

The trouble is that there are a great many poor managers. 'The supreme irony of business management is that it is far easier for an inadequate CEO to keep his job than it is for an inadequate subordinate,' lamented Buffett in 1988 going on to criticize the comfortable conspiracies of too many boardrooms. 'At board meetings, criticism of the CEO's performance is often viewed as the social equivalent of belching.'

Buffett's own leadership is characteristically down to earth. 'Charlie and I are the managing partners of Berkshire,' he explained in 1996. 'But we subcontract all of the heavy lifting in this business to the managers of our subsidiaries. In fact, we delegate almost to the point of abdication: Though Berkshire has about 33,000 employees, only twelve of these are at headquarters'. In fashionable books this would be called empowerment; to Buffett it is brazen common sense.

It is notable also that Buffett admits to mistakes and errors of judgment. After a long struggle, Berkshire was eventually forced to close down its original textile company. 'I should be faulted for not quitting sooner,' Buffett told shareholders, going out of his way to praise the efforts of the management: 'Every bit the equal of managers at our more profitable businesses'. Even good managers cannot save what has become a bad business. But it takes leadership to act on this.

As we were considering the leadership and investment style of Warren Buffett we were introduced to an idea from Dave Ulrich: the Leadership Capital Index. In many ways this is the missing link of investment.

'Wise, long-term investors recognize that leadership matters,' Ulrich explained to us with his customary gusto. His research found that investors allocate about 30 percent of their decision making on the quality of leadership.

Ulrich explains:

> Quality of leadership predicts intangible value which in turn produces financial results. But too often assessments of leadership are haphazard and narrow. Investors may say 'this leader is charismatic, has a vision, or treats people well' but there is little analysis behind what has become a 'gut feel' approach to assessment among many investors. Leadership assessments should go beyond isolated observations to more rigorous analytics. To move firm valuation discussions from financials to intangibles to leadership requires synthesizing massive studies and insights about leaders and leadership into a useable and simple leadership valuation solution.

In his book, *The Leadership Capital Index: Realizing the Market Value of Leadership*, Ulrich draws on a useful metaphor for how to include, conceive and audit leadership in the assessment of firm value. He explains that a leadership capital index is like a financial confidence index – Moody's or Standard & Poor's. It moves beyond casual and piecemeal observations of leaders to more thorough assessment of leadership.

'An index guides investors to make more informed choices,' says Ulrich. 'When a rating agency like Moody's or S&P downgrades a company, it is not saying the company did or did not meet financial reporting requirements. It is offering an opinion about the firm's ability to repay loans in the future. Likewise, a leadership capital index would inform investors about the readiness of the firm's leadership to meet business challenges.' Investment may never be the same again – even for Warren Buffett.

Resources

Dave Ulrich, *The Leadership Capital Index: Realizing the Market Value of Leadership* (Berrett Koehler, 2015).

Always learning   #26

A while ago one of us had a conversation with Joe Jimenez, CEO of the pharmaceutical company, Novartis. It was 4 July, a big day for Americans, but he was hard at work doing what a modern corporate leader does. What especially interested us about Jimenez was that he was an outsider to the pharma industry when he joined the company. He was not even a scientist when he became the head of the pharma division at Novartis in 2007.

We thought that it must have been awkward, indeed very difficult, dealing with the company's scientists, working at the leading edge of pharma, knowing nothing about the interior workings of molecules and so on. It was a point we made to Jimenez. 'I felt it was very important that I study not just our medicines but the diseases that our medicines are involved in, as well as the mechanism of the molecules that we have discovered and developed,' he agreed:

> I had a lot of help in understanding the science in the early years. I had a tutor that would come in early in the morning before the work day. We would pick a particular disease and he would explain how the disease progresses, what pathways are implicated in that disease and how the pieces manage through that disease and where each one of our compounds fit in the overall management of the disease.
>
> I found that with a lot of work, while sitting in meetings with our scientists, I was able to ask the right questions around what has been considered and what has not.

It is very interesting that you can run a company like this without being a physician or a scientist as long as you understand something about the sciences and you make sure that you have the right people in the room when you are debating. We have an innovation management board where there are some of the most brilliant scientists in the world sitting at the table as we are debating whether we are going to proceed to phase two or phase three on a particular program and I am in there with them. It is amazing how you can learn a new industry and learn the science even if you didn't grow up in that background.

Jimenez's willingness to go back to school, to put in the extra hours every single morning so he could hold his head up in a conversation struck us as entirely admirable, part perhaps of the humility we have seen in so many great leaders.

We are always suspicious of leaders who say they are not motivated by money – easy to say when you have a great deal of it. But, it is said to us so often, that we are becoming convinced that the very best leaders are driven by more laudable forces. This is how Chris Gibson-Smith, chairman of the London Stock Exchange, explained the motivation of his career: 'Making personal money is a consequence of my amused participation. I have followed my curiosity more than my ambition. And I think that's a more winding trail.'

Curiouser and curiouser. A similar appetite for improvement was expressed by the formidable Mick Davis, then CEO of Xstrata, when we spoke. Davis is a highly experienced business leader and yet, in our interview, he emphasized the need for continuing learning and development with and from colleagues. 'I continue to spend a lot of time trying to learn as much as I can about the qualities of the people in my business,' said Davis:

To do that, I travel to the various operations so I know who's there and what they're doing. Choosing the right people with the potential for success remains one of the key parts of my job. I spend a lot of time trying to encourage people to think about what they can do. I'm quite demanding in terms of outputs, but my style is one of very significant delegation of accountability and authority. Although I always think about risk, I am careful to allow people the space to get on with their jobs, make their own decisions, make their own mistakes – and learn from those mistakes. I also continue to try to be highly supportive when they run into trouble.

In their *Harvard Business Review* article, 'Are You a Good Boss or a Great One?', Linda Hill and Kent Lineback observe that a lot of bosses fail to fulfill their full potential because they neglect to continue developing their talents. They fail to ask the questions 'How good am I?' and 'Do I need to be better?' Hill and Lineback suggest that not enough bosses really know what is needed to be truly effective, or where they want to be in the future. Hill and Lineback suggest there are three imperatives which leaders face: to manage yourself, manage a network and manage a team.

Leaders need to influence others if they are to succeed. At the same time followers will be observing their boss at work, and making judgments about whether or not they are willing to let the leader influence them. The followers must trust their boss in order to be influenced. If trust comes from competence and character, leaders must manage themselves in ways that display competence and character and inspire trust.

Effective leaders manage their network well. Rather than recoiling from organizational politics, they embrace it, knowing that they need to make the right contacts in the organization if they are to exert influence in a productive way. Building an informal network throughout the organization, and engaging in organizational politics, is the best way to ensure they have the resources and power to get things done. Not only do effective leaders build and maintain these connections, they also make sure that they do it on several levels, including their own boss in the network, for example.

When you are leading a team, it can be tempting to deal with team members individually rather than collectively. Time is precious. Everyone is working hard. Online, virtual team meetings are not always that effective. Yet people like to be part of a team, to share common goals and feel that sense of collective purpose. Even if it is not the easiest option, an effective leader manages their team as a team and not as a group of individuals. Everyone needs to be included, and individuals will need to be dealt with individually, but that interaction can always be freehand in a team context.

Finally, the effective leader needs to keep tabs on how they are doing with the three imperatives. Fortunately, Hill and Lineback provide a checklist questionnaire to help them keep score.

The willingness to learn is not about signing up for evening classes – though these might be a good idea. It is an outlook on life, a willingness to listen and to learn from others, to admit fallibility rather than perpetuating the myth of leadership perfection.

Learning is also about having an appetite for reinvention. 'You can never have an impact on society if you have not changed yourself,' noted Nelson Mandela. There are second acts in leadership. There are comebacks. There are reinventions. Leaders are by their very nature curious and driven. This explains why the very best leaders have a capacity for the kind of reinvention which is beyond mere mortals.

Take the reinvention of Dame Ellen MacArthur. She remains best known for her remarkable sailing exploits. Aged 18 she set off to sail around the UK singlehandedly. She came second in the 2001 Vendée Globe solo round-the-world race and went on to break the world record for the fastest solo circumnavigation in 2005.

In the years following her world record, MacArthur remained involved in sailing. But, through her sailing experiences, visiting the remote island of South Georgia and having a powerful thirst for knowledge, MacArthur became fascinated by the economic and resource challenges facing the global economy. She announced her retirement from racing in 2009 and in 2010 launched the Ellen MacArthur Foundation.

MacArthur refers to the years before the establishment of the Foundation bearing her name as her 'journey of learning'. 'Being a round-the-world sailor is fairly specific in many ways – even though you have to learn many skills from understanding the weather to first aid to sailing,

I had absolutely no idea about global economics. It was a long journey of learning,' she told us when we talked at the Foundation's base, temptingly near to water.

Sailing around the world, every item on board has to justify its inclusion. The lighter the yacht, the faster. Each mouthful of food, each piece of kitchen roll has to be consumed with the overall resources in mind. Says MacArthur:

> On a boat you have finite resources and you really realize what finite means. Translate that to the global economy and you realize there are some pretty big challenges – 3.5 billion new middle-class consumers coming online, the population increasing, more and more demand on resources. We've seen a century of price declines erased in ten years. Economists don't seem to think that's going to change because there's more and more demand for commodities. And for me the question was, so what works?

With this question burning in her mind, MacArthur sought out answers. She visited a power station and saw the vast supplies of raw materials required to keep them running. She traveled, but with a new agenda. Her eyes were opened to the concept of the circular economy when she saw a diagram in a book by Ken Webster (later the Head of Innovation at the Foundation). 'Suddenly there was this idea of a cycle. For me it made sense. It was a different way of looking at things,' she says. 'I thought this could work. This is an economy that could run in the long term. At that stage we had absolutely no idea of the economics. It made sense from a materials flow perspective and it made sense from an energy perspective but we had no idea whether it cost three times more than a current linear product.'

MacArthur invested her own money for the first eighteen months to kickstart the Foundation. In straitened times it raised £6 million to fund its work into promoting understanding of what is now labeled the circular economy.

At the annual general meeting of the World Economic Forum in Davos in January 2015 the circular economy was one of the big ideas discussed and debated – thanks largely to Ellen MacArthur's campaigning work and her reinvention as a leader of ideas.

Resources

The interview with Joe Jimenez, 'Pharma plus', is in *Business Strategy Review* (Spring 2014).

Linda Hill and Kent Lineback's article, 'Are You a Good Boss or a Great One?', can be found in *Harvard Business Review*, 2011.

Ellen MacArthur's story is brilliantly told in *Full Circle* (Michael Joseph, 2010).

Leaders provide meaning

Talking with Stew Friedman, a professor at Wharton, we told him we'd been struck by the powerful strain of optimism in his work. 'Well, I'm glad that you picked that up,' he replied, 'because that is, to me, the hallmark of what leaders have to do; to convert the harsh realities of today into a hopeful path to make the world a little better. It is about looking at reality as clearly as you can and then, creatively, and in concert with other people, trying to figure out ways to improve the human condition.'

Leadership and progress are not one and the same, but they are so closely adjacent to mean that separating them would take clinical expertize. As Peter Drucker, the father of management thinking, famously observed, 'money is a by-product' of creating value and it is value which fuels progress in business and society.

'When you find your real purpose, you can pursue it with passion,' advises Unilever CEO Paul Polman.

'Leadership is about results,' says London Business School's Rob Goffee. 'It has to be. Great leadership has the potential to excite people to extraordinary levels of achievement. But it is not only about performance; it is also about meaning. This is an important point – and one that is often overlooked. Leaders at all levels make a difference to performance. They do so because they make performance meaningful.

'And the quest for meaning is increasingly important to societies and individuals. As the pace of change increases, individuals are ever more motivated to search for constancy and meaning. We've become increasingly suspicious of a world dominated by the mere role player.'

For Vineet Nayar of the Indian tech company HCL, faith-based organizations remain an inspiration. He envies their unifying sense of purpose. HCL has championed an emphasis on 'employees first' (also the title of Nayar's bestselling book). '*Employees First* energized the corporation. It made management accountable,' he says. 'But, today is what matters. Here and now. The human mind is not built for the past. The whole legacy thing is crap.' Belief is everything. Belief can change the world.

But meaning is about more than money. Take the design company IDEO. We have interviewed a variety of IDEO employees over the last decade, yet have never heard any mention of the usual corporate yardsticks – profits, ROI, market share. 'The business thing has always been an outcome of doing everything else we want to do rather than a sense of purpose in itself. If you're going to make a place good for creative people to come to, you don't make that a place that talks about business and money all the time,' IDEO CEO Tim Brown told us when we met in London:

> Creative people want to have an impact, they want to see their ideas out in the world making a difference to people, because that's why they went into the things that they do in the first place. Now that can include improving a business, absolutely, and nearly always does in fact. But in terms of our own business, we do good work, and we're constantly thinking about how what we do might evolve, and figuring out how to be as impactful as possible. The business seems to take care of itself.

Meaning leads to profits, not vice versa.

Visit the gleaming headquarters of the Japanese company Fujitsu in central Tokyo and the point is made abundantly, repeatedly and uncompromisingly clear. Technology exists – and matters – in order to make the world a better place. Societal and human improvement relies on technology. And so a technology company should be measured by the improvements in the world it brings about rather than the novelty value of its products, or simply its financial value.

Fujitsu is the world's fourth-largest IT services provider and number one in Japan. It talks about creating value through the integration of technology into our lives and businesses. Its practical vision of the role of technology finds its most powerful voice in the shape of its president Masami Yamamoto. A compact and serious-minded man, Yamamoto had a youthful interest in kendo ('the way of the sword'), an explosive but disciplined martial art, and, like many of his senior colleagues, has spent his entire career with the company.

'I am an engineer,' he says with engaging bluntness. It explains everything. The entire ethos of Masami Yamamoto and Fujitsu springs from this realization. It is a company built by engineers and, lest we forget, it was engineering excellence that transformed war-ruined Japan into an industrial powerhouse and, still to this day, the third biggest economy in the world.

With this come the preoccupations and fascinations of engineers. They seek out problems and apply their ingenuity to solving them. For that reason, Fujitsu's products and research are wide ranging. Once a social problem is solved, another one soon follows. Solving our societal problems is what the company does. That is why Fujitsu boasts about 100,000 patents worldwide and a $2.5 billion annual R&D budget. The impression is that the company's agenda is not set by simple money making, but by the interests and passions of the engineers combined with the input of consumers and the likely societal benefits of any project they work on.

Talk to other senior executives at Fujitsu and the engineering vision holds true. The company, with 162,000 employees operating in more than 100 countries, begins with engineering. But where does it go from there? What is its intended destination? Vice president Tango Matsumoto pauses to give a summary. 'I trust our people to maximize value for our customers. My ambition is doing well by doing good. We have to verify through our customers whether we are doing good or not.'

The job of the leader is to bring meaning to the organization and the performance of every single task in the organization. It is the classic story of whether a man is building a wall or helping to build a cathedral. Meaning builds.

Resources

Our interview with Stew Friedman can be found in *Leadership* (Mc-Graw Hill, 2013).

Our article on Fujitsu was in *Business Strategy Review* (Winter, 2014).

Leaders decide #28

Leaders make decisions and enable others to make them. Easier said than done.

'The essence of ultimate decision remains impenetrable to the observer – often indeed, to the decider himself … There will always be the dark and tangled stretches in the decision-making process – mysterious even to those who may be most intimately involved,' said John F. Kennedy.

There is an air of mystery which lies at the heart of decisions and decision making. An entire academic discipline, decision science, is devoted to understanding management decision making. Much of it is built on the foundations set down by early business thinkers who believed that under a given set of circumstances human behavior was logical and therefore predictable. The fundamental belief of the likes of computer pioneer Charles Babbage and Scientific Management founder Frederick Taylor was that the decision process (and many other things) could be rationalized and systematized. Based on this premise, models emerged to explain the workings of commerce which, it was thought, could be extended to the way in which decisions were made.

The belief in 'Decision Theory' persists. Indeed, most management books and ideas are inextricably linked to helping managers make better decisions. Strategic management, for example, was a model by which strategic decisions could be made. Unfortunately, it was a model which demanded vast amounts of data. As a result, enthusiastic managers turned themselves into data addicts rather than better decision makers.

Decisions were perpetually delayed as more data was gathered in order to ensure the decision would be 100 percent certain to work. 'Paralysis by analysis' became commonplace.

There is now a profusion of models, software packages and analytical tools which seek to distill decision making into a formula. Decision-making models assume that the distilled mass of experience will enable people to make accurate decisions. They enable you to learn from other peoples' experiences. Many promise the world. Feed in your particular circumstances and out will pop an answer. The danger is in concluding that the solution provided by a software package is the answer.

Whether in a software package or buried in a textbook, decision theorizing suggests that effective decision making involves a number of logical stages. This is referred to as the 'rational model of decision making' or the 'synoptic model'. The latter involves a series of steps – identifying the problem; clarifying the problem; prioritizing goals; generating options; evaluating options (using appropriate analysis); comparing predicted outcomes of each option with the goals; and choosing the option which best matches the goals.

Such models rely on a number of assumptions about the way in which people will behave when confronted with a set of circumstances. These assumptions allow mathematicians to derive formulae based on probability theory. These decision-making tools include such things as cost/benefit analysis, which aims to help managers evaluate different options.

Alluring though they are, the trouble with such theories is that reality is often more confused and messy than a neat model can allow for. Underpinning the mathematical approach are a number of flawed assumptions – such as that decision making is consistent; is based on accurate information; is free from emotion or prejudice; and is rational. Another obvious drawback to any decision-making model is that identifying what you need to make a decision about is often more important than the actual decision itself. If a decision seeks to solve a problem, it may be the right decision but the wrong problem.

The reality is that leaders make decisions based on a combination of intuition, experience and analysis. As intuition and experience are impossible to measure in any sensible way, the temptation is to focus on the analytical side of decision making, the science rather than the mysterious art. (The entire management consultancy industry is based on reaching decisions through analysis.) Of course, the leader in the real world does not care whether he or she is practicing an art or science. What they do care about is solving problems and reaching reliable, well-informed decisions.

This does not mean that decision theory is redundant or that decision-making models should be cast to one side. Indeed, a number of factors mean that decision making is becoming ever more demanding. The growth in complexity means that organizations no longer encounter simple problems. And complex decisions are now not simply the preserve of the most senior leaders but the responsibility of many others in organizations. In addition, leaders are having to deal with a flood of information – a survey by Reuters of 1,200 managers worldwide found that 43 percent thought that important decisions were delayed and that their ability to make decisions was affected as a result of having too much information.

These factors suggest that anything which enables leaders to make better informed decisions more quickly will be in increasing demand. They know that decisions are the lubricant which enables the engine of leadership to function.

Leadership jeans #29

It is the job of the leader to set standards. High ones.

One of the best examples of a leader seizing the initiative and shifting standards in an organization is that of the CEO of the Chinese white goods manufacturer Haier, Zhang Ruimin. In 1985, after receiving letters from consumers complaining about quality problems with Haier refrigerators, Zhang joined employees in demolishing seventy-six of the sub-standard refrigerators with sledgehammers. The point was made: Haier had to match or exceed the highest quality standards. The story is constantly referred to and one of the destroyed refrigerators remains on display in Haier HQ.

Such symbolic displays are hugely powerful but require constant reinforcement. There are few overnight successes in leadership or in organizations. Standards have to be set over time; values acquired, agreed upon and tested; examples set. Consider the story of Levi-Strauss & Co., one of the world's largest apparel companies with revenues nearing $5 billion and 16,000 employees. 'Next time you're in a Shanghai launderette, or a juke joint in Joliet, or a boardroom in midtown Manhattan, look for us. We'll be a simple, but essential, part of someone's individual style,' runs one company ad.

Not only is Levi's a top ranking global brand, it has got there the ethical way. The company has consistently won awards from public bodies and praise from business leaders for its commitment to ethics, values and social responsibility. In a poll of US business leaders, Levi-Strauss was voted the country's most ethical private company – an honor shared with the Merck Corporation, consistently recognized as America's most ethical public company.

At Levi-Strauss, ethics and values are not an afterthought, concepts bolted on to the business when economic success is guaranteed. They are at the core of its culture and are perceived to be key drivers of business success. The company manages its ethics and values commitments with the same degree of care and attention that it devotes to other critical business issues. As with John Lewis in the UK, Robert Bosch in Germany and Tata Industries in India, the company's commitment to good ethics and values was set by its founding family. But it has successfully transferred the family's personal commitment to ethics, values and social responsibility into its worldwide business ethos and management practices.

The importance of such historical commitment cannot be underestimated. A culture of ethics, values and social responsibility is built over time rather than overnight. The company has been a family-owned business for most of its 140-year history and this connection has been critical in shaping its sense of values and its brand. The Haas and Koshland families have influenced the ethics and values of Levi-Strauss.

The original Levi Strauss (1829–1902) came from Bavaria. He arrived in New York in 1847 and worked with his half-brothers in their dry goods business. In 1853 Strauss went to San Francisco to set up his own business. His big break came when one of his customers, a Nevada tailor called Jacob Davis, showed him an idea he had for riveting men's trousers. The result was robust and long lasting – suitable if you were a gold prospector or a farmer. Davis needed $68 to file a patent for the design. In 1873 Strauss and Davis patented the riveted trousers or 'waist-high overalls' as they were then called. The company prospered – when he died, Levi Strauss's estate was worth the then colossal amount of $6 million.

The first major challenge faced by the company occurred in 1906 when the San Francisco earthquake – followed by a fire – destroyed the company's headquarters and two factories. In response, Levi Strauss extended credit to its wholesale customers so they could get back on their feet and back in business. The company carried on paying its employees and a temporary office and showroom was opened to give them some work to do while a new HQ and factory were built.

A similar example was followed by the company during the Great Depression. The then CEO Walter Haas Sr. employed workers laying new floors at the company's Valencia Street plant in San Francisco rather than laying them off. Later, the company ensured equal employment opportunities for African-Americans in its factories during the 1950s and 1960s when expanding into the southern States. As the business grew the community involvement tradition developed alongside.

The trouble with leadership history lessons is that they can appear easy and almost preordained. But the leadership reality is that trust and ethics are fickle. Standards have to be maintained. While the 1960s saw Levi's reach international markets and become accepted as youth wear, the 70s were a different story. In the 1970s it was successfully prosecuted under Anti-Trust law in California. In 1971 the company went public. This proved highly unsuccessful. It also brought in a CEO from Playtex who encouraged it into brand extensions. Levi's swimwear, Levi's headgear and Levi's rainwear were among the best-forgotten diversions from the main business.

Between 1980 and 1984, the company's net income fell by over 80 percent. It shut or sold one quarter of its US factories and cut its workforce by 15,000 – nearly one third. 'The trust in the company and its leadership in particular was shattered,' reflected the man charged with rebuilding it, Robert D. Haas, the great-great grand-nephew of the founder. He took over as CEO in 1984 and successfully transmuted the company's benevolent paternalism into a more dynamic, modern approach to managing ethics and values, one which engages employees in the process.

Ethics remain an integral part of the company. The company published an 'aspirations statement' in 1987 which challenges all employees to show leadership in 'modeling new behaviors, empowerment, ethical management practices and good communications'. The Aspirations Statement also recognizes that people need recognition for their work and positive behavior, and commits the company to valuing and making good use of human diversity whether by age, race, sex or ethnic group. It is not decorative. Managers are not judged by economic performance alone. This is a critical message for the importance of these values to the company. Up to 40 percent of management bonuses are decided on performance measures relating to ethics, values and personal style in human relations as set out in the Aspirations Statement and elsewhere.

'We have told our people around the world what we value, and they will hold us accountable,' one Levi Strauss leader observed. 'Once you do that, it's like letting the genie out of the bottle. You can't go back.'

These lessons apply equally to leadership. Leaders have to clearly state what they value and welcome being held accountable for their performance.

Positively leadership   #30

Gianpiero Petriglieri, an Associate Professor of Organizational Behavior at INSEAD, trained as a psychiatrist before becoming an award-winning teacher and researcher whose work bridges the domains of leadership, adult development and experiential learning. 'I do a lot of work with senior executives and I always ask, how many of you stress because things aren't going in the direction you really wish them to go or aren't going there fast enough for you? And all of them raise their hands. Then I ask, how many of you beat yourself up for it, stand in front of the mirror and say, maybe that's because I'm not as good a leader as I should be? And all raise their hand again,' he says. 'We keep telling people that they can lead and be happy, but the reality of leadership is often different. Acknowledging the tension built into leadership may help get us leaders who are more capable of accepting limitations without losing aspiration.'

Leadership is difficult, demanding and draining. Successful leaders have developed survival strategies which enable them to survive the slings and arrows of leadership fortune. Physical and mental support and sustenance are increasingly part and parcel of leadership. Churchill made do with a cigar and a bottle of brandy; today's leaders are likely to have fitness and performance coaches. Research from Yahoo Finance found that 85 percent of CEOs say they exercise daily; 70 percent begin their day with a workout of some kind while 15 percent exercise between meetings or during a lunch hour. And the lunch hour may be a stretch: other research suggests that executives take an average lunch break of thirty-five minutes and work through lunch three days a week.

'After ten years working with business leaders, one clear thing I've learned is that sustainable high performance can only be created when you integrate daily strategies in four areas: mindset, nutrition, movement and recovery,' says Scott Peltin, co-author of *Sink, Float, or Swim*, chief performance officer at Tignum and a former firefighter:

> How focused, confident, empathetic, or open are you when you are exhausted, over-stressed, sleep deprived, starving, or even after sitting all day without moving? Just as in executing your business strategy, your personal performance strategy is loaded with choices you will face every day where you will either become more of a sustainable high performer or less. It's a no-brainer: think of the benefits (at work and at home) of making significantly better choices.

Given all these demands, it is just as well that leaders tend to have a positive outlook. Indeed, all the successful leaders we have encountered have a positive and optimistic view of the world. They are not unrealistic, but simply prefer to see the glass as half full rather than half empty. As Napoleon observed: 'A leader is a dealer in hope'.

'I'm very optimistic,' Sir Peter Lampl told us. 'My experience of business is that most people, if properly motivated, led and incentivized, will do a good job. All the companies I bought were underperforming businesses, losing money or making poor returns. I didn't go in and fire a bunch of people, because most people will do a good job. What I tried to do is to help them do a better job. And I think that's what we've got to do with teachers.'

Positivity is much in vogue thanks to the rise of positive psychology. Now, it is increasingly applied to leadership. Among those in the vanguard of positive leadership is Lee Newman of Spain's IE Business School. He suggests a new approach to leadership designed to achieve behavioral advantage – 'an advantage achieved by building an organization of individuals and teams that think and perform better, at all levels'. In his positivity armory are such things as yoga and mindfulness.

Sustainable competitive advantage is no longer attainable in the conventional sense, argues Newman, a former tech entrepreneur and

McKinsey & Co consultant. However, it is possible to obtain behavioral advantage. This can be done, he contends, by taking the latest research and thinking in behavioral economics and positive psychology, and applying it to improve individual and organizational performance.

According to Newman, there are three main elements to positive leadership. The first is mindware training which helps leaders understand their decision-making thought processes, and enables them to think better. The second element focuses on building up people's strengths, rather than on improving their weaknesses. Companies should be, says Newman, 'identifying the strengths of their people and teams and then designing the work around them. It's a win–win: better for the wellbeing of employees and better for the bottom line of the organization.'

The third aspect of positive leadership that the leader needs to attend to is professional fitness. Leaders must ensure that they and their followers apply their learning in their everyday work.

There are, of course, skeptics who suggest that leaders should by their very nature be able to look after themselves. This is true up to a point. But it is clear that leadership demands physical and mental fortitude and dexterity. These can and must be worked at in order to improve.

'I have pursued the idea that the solution to the work/life dilemma is leadership and that the heart of leadership is really the whole person,' says Stew Friedman, Practice Professor of Management at the Wharton School of the University of Pennsylvania. He trained as an organizational psychologist, was founding director of the Wharton Leadership Program and is also founding director of Wharton's Work/Life Integration Project. 'You can advance your leadership capacity, performance and results at work and elsewhere by bringing together the different parts of your life; integrating them in an intelligent way that works for you. Behind this is the notion that each person can emerge as more of a leader than he or she currently is. And that leadership can be learned, practiced and developed, like any performing art or a sport, even if it cannot be taught.'

What is clear is that leadership is not an occasional act or something requiring only part of your brain and energy. It is demanding, yes, but demanding of the whole person rather than a neat compartment marked 'leadership'. Because of this, looking after the whole person is essential for healthy and effective leadership.

Resources

We are long-term fans of the work of Stew Friedman. To find out more about his work look up www.totalleadership.org.

Lee Newman's website is www.leenewman.com.

Slow leadership   #31

In 1984 executives at Coca-Cola were worried. The company appeared to be on the edge of a terrible precipice. Its number one place in the coke market appeared under genuine threat for the first time. Pepsi was catching up fast. Market share was slipping – Coca-Cola was reduced to a market share lead of just less than 5 percent. Coca-Cola's ad spend was up but was having little effect. Pepsi had come up with a good ad play for a number two in the market: the Pepsi Challenge. The Challenge had led to a sharp increase in Pepsi's market share – up an immediate 8 percent. Trouble was, the Pepsi Challenge was more than a gimmick. In blind tests it seemed that drinkers actually did prefer Pepsi to Coca-Cola. This was not good news for the Coca-Cola marketing team.

Faced with these problems, Coca-Cola charged Sergio Zyman with a project to consider the previously unthinkable: changing the drink's recipe.

In September 1984 the Coca-Cola team came up with a recipe which, in blind tests, kept on winning. This, the company concluded, was the answer. However, it conveniently ignored consistently negative market research about the possibility of changing the drink's formula. Coca-Cola went for it. On 23 April 1985 New Coke was announced – on St George's Day, the dragon came out to slay Pepsi.

New Coke was claimed to be smoother, sweeter and preferable to the old version. This conveniently overlooked the fact that the old version was selling in many millions every day of the week. To call this the marketing own-goal of the century would be to understate the effect only slightly. Coke was faced with a barrage of criticism. On the other hand, its arch-rival Pepsi could barely contain its glee – indeed, it quickly produced advertising which was extremely gleeful, rubbing in the fact that 'the real thing' remained unchanged.

Realizing that its move had been disastrous, Coke back-tracked and, after ninety days, reintroduced the original coke. It has not been tinkered with since.

So, what does this salutary saccharined tale have to offer twenty-first century leaders?

First, if it works, don't change it without a very good reason. There was more to Coca-Cola than the recipe. It stood for something. And the company underestimated how strong this bond was.

Second, learn, don't blame. It was notable that the Coca-Cola top management team remained in place and did so for a number of years. Heads did not roll. Indeed, Robert Goizueta, the CEO, received $1.7 million in salary and bonuses. The company's annual statement noted 'singular courage, wisdom and commitment in making certain decisions'. It might have been different if the company had lost money. The company's stock actually reached an all-time high at the beginning of 1986.

Third, we all make mistakes. Coca-Cola recognized its folly quickly and acted decisively. Its followers forgave.

The Coke story is a business classic, but it came back to us when Stuart was recounting his experiences over twenty-three days in the company of four other middle-aged men on a 38-foot yacht crossing the Atlantic Ocean. Since returning, people have been asking him what he learned along the way. It is interesting – and a relatively recent phenomenon – that you are expected to learn something in any unusual experience. The experience in itself is not enough; you must have actively learned something from it. As one of his crewmates (a CEO, as it turns out) observed: 'Twenty odd days on a boat in the middle of nothingness and I still haven't figured out the meaning of life.'

You do, of course, learn things in any twenty-three-day period in life and on a boat in the middle of the ocean. But the process of learning is as ad hoc as it normally is: learning is gradually acquired rather than arriving in dramatic and sizeable lightning bolts. Learning happens and evolves.

It is your willingness to accept and embrace the slowness and granularity of the process which is key.

This also applied to the brand of leadership Stuart encountered while on board. The captain was a former headteacher. His modus operandi was to allow you to give something a try and then intercede with some helpful advice as the rope failed to move, the sail continued to flap or the gas didn't ignite.

Good theory, but it is amazing how challenging that approach actually is. It feels like low-key, educational leadership, but for the person being given the opportunity to try something and, in Stuart's case, almost certainly fail to do it, the pressure is intense. He could feel the faith the captain was putting in him every time. He wanted to be able to do it. And he could feel the specter of failure hovering.

The truth is that Stuart is not used to failure. His adult life has been spent deliberately putting himself in situations where he can utilize the skills and insights he has. It is good, he knows, to get out of your comfort zone. But that is not how most people spend their personal and professional lives. You don't want to be the one person who can't do something, you don't want to repeatedly get things wrong, you don't want to fail – especially in front of others.

His captain's leadership also had an interesting safety mechanism. When it was suggested that he might do something – let a reef out so the sail was bigger and the boat would go faster, put the genoa up, change tack and so on – his reaction was often to say no. 'Good idea, but let's wait twenty minutes and see what the wind is doing then,' he would say, in a positively-negative tone honed in the classroom.

When he said such things the crew would glance at each other, roll their eyes slightly and think to themselves that the captain was a great guy but not a fearless and quick decision maker.

They were, of course, wrong. After twenty minutes, time after time, the situation was completely different from the one they had imagined.

Taking a reef out or putting a sail up would have been ill advised and sometimes dangerous.

Partly this was down to experience. The captain had been in more similar situations so he was able to make the right call. But, more importantly, the captain repeatedly got decisions right because he pressed pause and went with the status quo while he weighed things up.

Of course, the natural suspicion is that this brand of slow leadership wouldn't work in the fast-moving organizational world. But the weather changes very quickly in the ocean. Before making any decision, a leader is well advised to press pause and consider whether the change will definitely improve performance and to consider the motives of those advising change. Slow leadership is often the quickest way forward – ask Coke.

Resources

Stuart is also author of a collection of poems entitled *Atlantic Crossing* (St Giles Poets, 2015).

Leaders are talent magnets #32

'In our business, it's very difficult to motivate people simply by money. You cannot,' Vivek Singh, head chef and CEO of the Cinnamon Club restaurant chain, told us:

A chef might earn £20,000 a year. For that, he works forty, fifty, sixty hours sometimes, a week, in a very hot environment. If I was relying on money as a motivator, I would never be able to build a team. So we're big on our values, what makes us different, what makes us unique, why do we do things differently? When we say 'how about doing it like this?' or 'why are you doing it like this?', the common answer is 'because it's easier'. Often that's not the right answer, because if it's easy, that's not good enough.

I say to the guys, there's two things I can give you. One is I can give you knowledge. Nothing is secret, everything is open. And I can give you respect.

For Vivek Singh developing the people in his team is core to his leadership. 'You can grow yourself, you're good, you follow instructions, you do things the way you're told. But how can you have the same effect on the people below you, so we're all constantly pulling and bringing people up? It's a slightly different skill to growing yourself. But to bring other people up to the next level, that's the challenge I see, from here onwards. It will be about those people who can spot talent and see the potential in something.'

Unconsciously, Vivek Singh was echoing the observation of that doyen of leadership thinking, Niccolo Machiavelli: 'The first method for estimating the intelligence of a ruler is to look at the men he has around him.' He was right.

Talking to a Silicon Valley VC we asked what he was looking for when he met up with an entrepreneur with a fledgling business in need of investment. His answer was simple. He didn't especially look for particular character traits or personalities. Experience had told him that all shapes and sizes of entrepreneurs with lots of different personalities succeeded and, anyway, gauging personality is notoriously difficult. What he looked for was who were the entrepreneur's first hires. If they hired someone who looked to all intents and purposes out of their league this was a good sign. If they attracted a couple of unexpectedly great people, even better.

We talked to David Pyott when he was CEO of Allergan, the company that brought Botox to the world, headquartered in Irvine, California. 'A strong leader must surround him or herself with very strong people. We have a very strong management team. If people don't keep growing, at some point they'll be asked to leave and I think the board is the same. I'm not looking for an easy ride,' said Pyott.

The entrepreneur Brent Hoberman (co-founder of lastminute.com) told us much the same:

> You want to invest in amazingly smart people, and sometimes even if they've got slightly the wrong idea, one should just back them because they'll get the right idea. They'll pivot and find it. And I don't think I've always been brutal enough in my investment strategy. Sometimes I could say, that idea is brilliant, I could see myself using it. But there have been a few good examples of where somebody else has made it happen, not the company I've invested in. That's because the entrepreneurs probably didn't have the passion, the tenacity. I look for people who are really savvy and sharp.
>
> A key question is: what does employee number ten look like? Is the idea exciting enough that employee number ten is going to be a really exceptional individual?

A follow-up question, Hoberman suggests, is 'Would I work for this person?'

And it is much the same with leaders. The best leaders attract great, talented people who want to change the world by working for the leader and the organization.

'We look for a particular profile,' Joe Jimenez, the CEO of Novartis told us. 'Some scientists look at Novartis coming in from academia and they want to pursue the science, not necessarily to develop new drugs. We screen those people out. We want people to pursue being a scientist but we want people who fundamentally want to move from an academic environment to discover new drugs that will help patients.'

Describing the new breed of leaders, Warren Bennis observed:

> They are connoisseurs of talent, more curators than creators. The leader is rarely the best or the brightest in the new organizations. The new leader has a smell for talent, an imaginative Rolodex, is unafraid of hiring people better than they are. In my research into great groups I found that in most cases the leader was rarely the cleverest or the sharpest. Peter Schneider, president of Disney's colossally successful Feature Animation studio, leads a group of 1,200 animators. He can't draw to save his life. Bob Taylor, former head of the Palo Alto Research Center, where the first commercial PC was invented, wasn't a computer scientist. Max DePree put it best when he said that good leaders 'abandon their ego to the talents of others.'

Not only do the best leaders attract the best, they also develop them – that is part of the bargain. Think back to Vivek Singh and his chefs. 'Leadership is not defined by the exercise of power but by the capacity to increase the sense of power of those being led. The most essential work of the leader is to create more leaders,' observed the early management thinker Mary Parker Follett. The key question any leader should ask is how they are creating the next generation of leaders in their team or organization.

Leaders work on weaknesses   #33

Education systems and upbringing tend to encourage us to identify what we excel at and then to work on that. We become more specialized, more focused. Along the way, it is easy to forget about, or totally overlook, our weaknesses. It is, perhaps, human nature to accentuate the positive, after all.

What you are perceived to be bad at is quickly identified and ingrained. A joke is made of your ineptitude at basic math. You are deemed a geek rather than being arty. You are a practical person rather than a thinker. All of these conclusions may be correct, but they instantly mean that you are unlikely ever to tackle your weaknesses.

And so we concentrate on fine tuning our strengths, becoming geekier, ever more practical, creative or whatever our flair is for. But there are times when this blind focus on honing what we are already good at can actually get in the way of our development.

In business, in particular, this is true. The people who become CEOs often have a particular expertise. That might be in finance, marketing, accounting or another area. But, in addition to this specific expertise, almost all successful business leaders have much broader experience. They may have worked throughout the world, run different function areas in the company. Broad general knowledge is what gets you to the top in business.

One of the most inspiring leaders we have encountered is Vineet Nayar who was CEO of the Indian technology company HCL. He told us how the global slowdown from 2008 had played straight into HCL's responsive hands:

> So you are the team which rows in still waters better than anybody else. That's fine. Now suddenly there's turbulence, and you need to do river rafting. Most companies keep crying that the environment is not good for rowing – our rowing skills are not being used and we're waiting for the environment to settle down so we can row again. No. Managers cannot be married to what they are good at. They have to be good at what the environment seeks from them. Otherwise they should step out of the way and let somebody else do what is required. The time is to river raft, to start intuitively driving the boat, and there is an opportunity. At HCL we need to become the best river rafter in town.

The trouble is that managers tend to carry on doing what they have always done. It got them there in the first place.

To carry on the water metaphor, one person we came across who started winning when he acknowledged and began working on his weaknesses is the Olympic gold medal winner and five times world champion rower Alex Gregory.

Rowing is a demanding sport. It requires large amounts of technique, strength and endurance, as well as team work. Gregory rows in a team of four or eight. His early career was bedeviled by injury and ill health. He under-performed at the big events. Just before the Beijing Olympics in 2008 he fractured a rib and so was out of the British team. He was chosen as the squad's reserve and so attended the Games. Watching the action unfold changed his career. He told us:

> It was a magical time, a revelation and without doubt the most influential time period in my rowing career. I was a spectator watching the people I had trained with seven days a week, 364 days a year for seven years, perform spectacularly. I was full of contrasting emotions: pride to have been part of this team, jealousy that they were doing what I so badly wanted to do, and surprisingly motivated to give it all one last try.

The moment of realization was sudden and powerful. All these years, after each disappointment the answer had always been to get back on the river, refine my skills and glide ever closer to the Holy Grail of perfect technique. But sitting there in the stands with the national anthem playing in the background I realized I had only ever been working on my strengths and overlooking my weaknesses. I was confident that I could have been in any of those gold-medal-winning boats from any nation and not upset the balance. But, watching these athletes closely I realized the problem lay elsewhere: I simply wasn't strong enough.

Alex Gregory's realization was career changing. He is not alone. Concentrating on honing your strengths and not identifying or tackling your weaknesses is commonplace. This applies to the tennis player who habitually avoids using a weak backhand; the CEO who is great with numbers, but doesn't begin to understand how marketing works; the teacher who knows a subject inside out but is not so good at classroom discipline.

'The problem is that it is so easy to work on what you are already good at. There is instant satisfaction and positive feedback with an often false belief that large steps have been made in the right direction. In fact the likelihood is that the rate of improvement is small and relatively insignificant. You do something well and strive every sinew to do it ever so slightly better. The belief is that accentuating your strengths offsets your weaknesses,' says Gregory. 'We are encouraged as parents and teachers that positive feedback is good and the right thing to do. This is great and something I completely agree with but it means that from a very early age we are all looking for this positive stimulus from others around us. We achieve this by doing and repeating actions we are good at, doing them well, making them better. The trouble is that this simply moves us even further away from what we really need to be doing to make significant changes.'

Returning home, Gregory spent the next three months locked in the gym. His target was to put on eight kilograms of muscle. He doubled his calorie and protein intake, set himself an intense weights program and within one month was seeing significant strength improvements. It took three months for him to reach his target.

For Alex Gregory the pay off was immediate. He started to beat those who had always beaten him before and soon he was chosen for the coxless four – GB Rowing's flagship boat. In 2009 he became World Champion, his first ever international medal, and in 2012 won an Olympic gold.

'At a personal level, working on my weaknesses radically changed my performance,' concludes Alex Gregory. 'Years of disappointment also toughened me. There are so many tasks in every walk of life that could be achieved faster, simpler and with less expense if some basic principles were met.'

Resources

An interview with Alex Gregory can be seen on the *Harvard Business Review* website. His own website is www.alexgregory.co.uk

Leaders collaborate #34

The chef Vivek Singh arrived in London – for the first time – with his small team of chefs in December 2000. 'All of the people who worked with me moved. It was a journey, an exciting change from doing a certain kind of cooking that everybody else was doing, to something that only we would be doing.' On 21 March 2001 the Cinnamon Club restaurant opened its doors to the public with Singh and his team at the helm.

Prior to accepting the job, Singh had never previously visited the UK. Suddenly, he was involved in the launch of a restaurant right in the heart of London and one which was making claims to revolutionize the eating experience. 'In many ways ignorance is bliss. I never really thought about whether it would succeed or not. Naivety! I had nothing to lose,' says Singh. 'I wanted to cook, I wanted to do more, and more. And the more you do, the more you want to do.' In three months Singh had to figure out the groundbreaking food to accompany the groundbreaking customer experience. He had to discover suppliers in a strange city and much more.

Vivek Singh arrived in London with a team of five chefs. Two more were added for the Cinnamon Club's launch. That team now is twenty strong. Of the eight people in the original kitchen, six are still with the group. In an industry famed for its high staff turnover, the 125 Cinnamon employees remain exceptionally loyal.

Leadership is inextricably caught up with individualism, but the reality is that leaders need teams. Leadership is teamwork.

Wharton's Katherine J. Klein spent ten months studying medical teams in action at the Shock Trauma Center in Baltimore. Her close up view of leadership in action led her to adopt a unique perspective on leadership 'as a system or a structure – a characteristic not of individuals but of the organization or unit as a whole'. Leadership is reconstrued in this world view as a dispersed activity rather than the monopoly of individuals.

In the fraught, pressured conditions that the trauma unit worked in, where poor decisions or wasted seconds might mean the difference between life and death, leadership was 'a role – or, more specifically, a dynamic, socially enabled and socially constrained set of functions which may be filled by the numerous individuals who, over time, occupy key positions of expert authority on the team'.

In such a situation leadership was the product of the organization or unit's 'norms, routines and role definitions'. The function of the leader existed separately from the many different people who fulfilled the role depending on the circumstances.

Klein identified four key leadership functions: providing strategic direction; monitoring team performance; instructing team members; and providing hands-on assistance when required.

Based on Klein's findings, organizations should put in place the structures needed to support whoever steps into a leadership position – have well established roles and clearly identified norms – rather than concentrate on selecting brilliant leaders.

Truly dispersed and fairly distributed leadership is unusual. More obviously attainable, perhaps, is the notion of collaborative leadership which Herminia Ibarra and Morten Hansen of INSEAD have looked at. 'No company has all the resources that it needs in-house, so we have to work across boundaries. That is the essence of collaborative leadership, simply mobilizing and inspiring people to get great results working across boundaries,' says Ibarra (who won the Leadership Award at the 2013 Thinkers50). 'What kind of leadership allows organizations to identify interesting collaborative opportunities, to bring the best talents to those opportunities, and then to lead the process so that it gets to an effective result? Collaborative leadership is far removed from the traditional command and control model.'

Ibarra identifies several areas that leaders need to focus on to become good collaborative leaders. To start with they need to build networks that allow them to add value collaboratively through connections. Leaders should also engage diverse talent from a broad range from the periphery. 'That periphery could be other geographies, other nationalities, generational, bringing other people into the discussion, gender diversity, it could be many things,' she says.

Establishing conditions conducive to the collaborative process comes next. That includes eradicating any politics and turf wars that might obstruct collaboration. 'You have to role model that from the top; if you don't have your collaborative potential at the top it just does not happen.'

And lastly, says Ibarra, show a strong hand. There is no call for collaboration on everything. A constant need for consensus can kill collaboration. Instead, the collaborative leader knows when to step back and when to take action to keep collaboration moving forward and adding value.

And, in order to master collaborative leadership, leaders will have to disavow themselves of some commonly held on views on leadership. Take situational leadership, and the need for command and control leadership in certain situations, for example.

'This idea of situational leadership is really ingrained,' says Ibarra. 'People believe that when times are good they can do all the good things, they can let go, they can collaborate infinitely. But when times are hard, it is time to close ranks, now you have to direct and control. That is not true. When times are tough, that's when we need ideas, that's when we need to reach out further. I think that is the real barrier, the sense that there is time for each, and command and control is still the answer to tough times.'

Resources

Herminia Ibarra and Morten Hansen's article 'Are you a collaborative leader?' can be found in *Harvard Business Review*, July–August 2011.

Zoom in, zoom out   #35

One of the most inspiring leaders we have ever met is Dame Ellen MacArthur. Her work with the Ellen MacArthur Foundation is a long way from her exploits when she was one of the world's greatest sailors.

'Something that I learnt through sailing was to look at the big picture,' she told us. 'When you're sailing a boat around the world you're not just looking at the boat speed and the waves around you, you're looking at what's coming in two hours, two days, two weeks. You're looking at how far north or south you want to be, you're looking at the sea temperature, the depth of the water, the five hundred charts to see what the weather's doing. To understand where you are in this you need to see the big picture.'

The organizational world with its myriad of differing agendas and priorities represents an enormous change from the certainties – albeit dangerous ones – of racing from A to B in a yacht or sailing around the world in the fastest time. 'Yes, but it's just a different racecourse,' counters MacArthur. 'The winner of the race is not necessarily the fastest sailor. The winner of the race is someone who is a fast sailor but is also able to keep the boat on track, maintain their energy levels throughout three months, is able to look at and understand the weather, make the decisions, repair the boat, repair themselves. It's a whole range of skills.'

Ellen MacArthur is a master of many skills, but one of the clearest is one which is central to modern leadership: being able to move from the short term to the long term – constantly. Leaders have to master the art of zooming in and zooming out at the right times.

'I have to ruthlessly manage my calendar because I am always deep in meetings,' Novartis' Joe Jimenez told us:

> In any thirty-minute time period there are literally three different meetings that I should be in and I have to pick one. I spend a lot of my time trying to balance between short-term decisions that have to be made and the longer-term strategic decisions that we are making that put the company on a certain course.
>
> I can't abdicate my role of delivering the results every year and every quarter but, at the same time, I have to be involved in the key decisions that set this big aircraft carrier on a course. That means from a very early stage I have to start shaping those longer-term decisions.'

The long and short terms are powerfully mixed at the fast growing Indian company Infosys. Its leaders appear skilled in zooming in to tackle the nitty-gritty of delivering complex projects and zooming out to look at the broader picture.

'If you're really serious about client value then it's not only about short-term value, it's about long-term value, you have to understand where would the clients go to over time and how are we prepared,' says Sanjay Purohit who joined the company in 2000. 'I am not working for a company, per se, I'm not in a job, I'm actually building something which is of value to our clients, it's of value to our employees, it's of value to our shareholders. Way back in 2000, perhaps 2001, I stopped working for Infosys and I started working with Infosys.'

The zooming in and out mantra was also echoed by Vodafone's Vittorio Colao. 'I really have two extremes,' he said:

> One is deep on facts, analysis, numbers, reports and all those things. I have a very good memory, so I am able to say to a manager, 'This is not what you told me in our meeting one year ago when I was here in Turkey: how come?' Second, I am able to gather quick impressions about what's happening, what the trends are and how an organization is functioning. I move around a great deal, getting impressions from people and from facts. Seeing me going around in shops, talking to everybody, stopping at coffee machines – my colleagues would think that my style is random, but it's not random at all.

127

The art of swooping down into the detail had also been mastered by David Pyott, then CEO of Allergan:

> I like to take quick and rather dramatic decisions. I've got better at settling back and letting other people come forward with ideas. We've all seen despotic organizations where everybody lives in fear of the CEO and nobody does anything until he tells them. We're not that kind of place. I tend to push things down a lot, but I've got really good measurement systems and know what's going on so I can suddenly descend from 50,000 feet down to about five inches. I think people like that, but some find it frightening.

Research of more than 10,000 executives in over 1,000 organizations throughout the world by Andrew and Nada Kakabadse suggests that the effective global leader is adept – almost mechanically so – at moving in and out of contexts, cultures and characters. They call this zooming in and out. Think of a zoom lens on a camera; it allows the operator to pull back and see the big picture but it also allows them to zoom in on the detail. Like a skillful photographer, the best leaders move from big picture to nitty-gritty detail – switching perspective many times within the same conversation or meeting.

'Among the hundred of boards we have studied, we have observed that the ability to zoom in and out in a measured and skillful way is one of the characteristics that mark out exceptional leaders – be they chairmen or chief executives,' the Kakabadses explain. 'In many cases, they use their zoom lens to probe and uncover the true issues that need to be resolved, separating the personalities from the policies and the cultural nuances from the business context. In this way the most effective chairman or CEO is able to tease out the real issues and resolve problems to make things happen.'

The Kakabadses' research suggests leaders do this in three distinct domains: the characters they are dealing with; the context of the meeting; and the culture in which they are operating. Each of these domains ranges from big picture level to the highly granular nitty-gritty level. Andrew Kakabadse explains:

Take the character domain, for example. A CEO might look around the boardroom table and see the bigger picture of the characters there – viewing them as their job title: the CFO, CTO for Europe and global HR director. But when required they can also zoom in to see them as individuals – Susan, David and Pablo, with all their human, idiosyncratic ways. How does this work in practice? In contemplating the CTO's negative response to a proposal, the CEO zooms in on his character. He remembers that David was overlooked for promotion last year and is still sore about it. That knowledge may allow the CEO to unlock David's response to persuade him to support the idea on the table, perhaps with a gentle reminder that the project will create a new role of global CTO that he would be well qualified to fill.

Surprisingly, too, the ability to zoom in and out is not as common as you might imagine. Many highly competent leaders we have studied have a weakness – or blind spot – in this area.

Andrew and Nada Kakabadse's research suggests that most leaders have a default or preferred setting. They either lean towards the zoom out position – often characterized as big picture thinkers – or they like to zoom in, and are characterized as the nitty-gritty guys or dealers in detail. They are capable of zooming in and out on occasions, but they do not do so automatically.

But there is a third group of executives with a very different style. These leaders are highly adept at zooming in and out during the course of a meeting, or in any other situation where they exercise their leadership. Having observed their behavior over many years, we have found that these individuals are far more effective at getting their desired outcomes from meetings and other management situations. They make excellent chairmen and chairwomen. They are more effective at creating buy-in and identifying and fixing problems before they become a block on organizational effectiveness. In short, they reap the profits of zoom.

Resources

Andrew Kakabadse, *The Success Formula* (Bloomsbury, 2015).

Leaders thrive on ambiguity

'To be omnipotent but friendless is to reign,' wrote Percy Bysshe Shelley. He was right. Even if a leader's power doesn't quite stretch to omnipotence, being a leader can be a lonely place. Isolation and ambiguity are powerfully destructive forces among the ranks of leaders.

In 1985 *Leaders: The Strategies for Taking Charge* was published, co-authored by Warren Bennis with Burt Nanus, founder and director of the Center of Futures Research at the University of Southern California. The book is based on research examining the lives of ninety of America's best-known leaders. The eclectic mix of names included McDonald's founder Ray Kroc and many other people from the worlds of business, sports, the arts – even an astronaut called Neil Armstrong.

'They were right-brained and left-brained, tall and short, fat and thin, articulate and inarticulate, assertive and retiring, dressed for success and dressed for failure, participative and autocratic,' says Bennis. But despite the diversity, they were united in one thing at least, they have all shown 'mastery over present confusion'.

And the confusion is real and permanent. Dame Mary Marsh, who has led schools and major not-for-profit organizations, says: 'One of the surprising things is how, at the time, you make decisions and you always make them on imperfect information. You look back and wonder how on earth you did that. But in any situation there is a strategic response to how you should move things forward and there are a range of options.

Some may be slightly better than others. What really matters is how you implement what you decide to do.'

Liz Mellon of Duke Corporate Education and author of *Inside the Leader's Mind: Five Ways to Think Like a Leader*, offers a different perspective on authenticity in leadership: 'There's a whole lot of ambiguity and complexity out there in the world. Imagine you are running a business that spans multiple countries, with thousands of employees, and all the complexity that goes with that, markets, politics, national cultures. Somehow you have to live with that, find a way through it, and still have the courage to take the decisions that need to be taken, while being comfortable with the level of complexity that's coming at you.'

We were struck talking to one CEO who told us that he only became fully aware of the nature of the job when he had to make a multi-million-dollar decision about an IT system. He had an IT team. It had all been costed very carefully and the experts were advising that it was a necessary investment. But he realized that the buck stopped at his desk and he needed to trust the advice he was given and make a decision to go ahead without fully understanding what he was agreeing to.

Such situations are commonplace for many leaders. Sometimes the leader has huge amounts of data to support their decision making – whether they should go into Argentina, get out of Chile, or change personnel. Sometimes there's no data at all.

For leaders coping with that kind of complexity it is difficult not to convey the pressure to others – inside and outside the organization. 'Exactly,' says Liz Mellon. 'The leaders have to live with that uncertainty, and with a smile on their face, so that they are not worrying everybody else around them with the level of ambiguity they are actually coping with, day in, day out.' Grin and bear it.

Resources

Liz Mellon's *Inside the Leader's Mind* is a book we recommend. For more on Liz's work please visit www.lizmellon.com.

Leaders look good   #37

A while ago we were running a session on leadership at an Ivy League business school. We showed a clip of someone. He looks like a leader, the group purred. We pushed them, but they struggled to go beyond this observation. The person in question was what would commonly be thought of as good looking. But we actually knew him, and he had no interest at all in being a leader. He looked like a leader, but he wasn't one.

The look of a leader is an interesting idea. 'Marvelous is the power which can be exercised, almost unconsciously, over a company, or an individual, or even upon a crowd by one person gifted with good temper, good digestion, good intellects and good looks,' wrote the novelist Anthony Trollope.

How a leader looks is closely tied to how we react to them. But it is not simply a question of being good looking. After all, many of the most influential leaders in history would not have fitted into that particular category. This brings us to that most elusive of leadership qualities: charisma, originally a Greek word meaning gift. In the New Testament charisms were gifts bestowed by Holy Spirit. These charismatic gifts included wisdom, knowledge, faith, the ability to perform miracles or speak in tongues; they also include gifts intended to be used to organize and build the church.

Max Weber, the German sociologist, philosopher and political economist, took up the notion of charisma as a source of authority and legitimacy. He used it to describe a situation where authority is not derived from rules or position, but instead from a 'devotion to the specific and exceptional sanctity, heroism, or exemplary character of an individual person, and of the normative patterns or order revealed or ordained by him.'

In Weber's view, charisma was associated with times of crisis. People in trouble look to charismatic leaders – with their characteristic sense of mission and destiny, their zeal and purpose – to lead them to safety.

The nature and characteristics of charisma were investigated by sociologists and political scientists for many years. Characteristics variously associated with charismatic leaders included an overarching vision and ideology, heroic acts and the ability to inspire, for example. There was a view held by some researchers that charismatic leadership was a relational concept and dependent on the perspective of followers.

Margarita Mayo of IE Business School, who has researched charismatic leadership over the last twenty years, believes that charismatic leaders gain influence by changing the way their followers think about themselves – and this goes for charismatic bosses and their employees as well. 'Leadership charm enables people to feel better about themselves and their own potential,' she says.

Mayo's research suggests that charismatic leaders help their believers do the following things:

Build self-esteem

The charismatic leader emphasizes the contribution of each individual and how he or she can play an important role in society and serve as a critical resource to the overall project. Followers undergo a personal transformation, beyond their own expectations, which leads to stronger self-esteem and self-worth.

Provide a sense of community

Charismatic leaders keep us from feeling that we are alone, and help us see that we belong to a community that promotes change and transformation. This sense of belonging is a powerful tool that channels individual complaints and personal goals into an organized group that works for common values and the good of the collective. During crises, charismatic leaders provide the necessary social cohesion that lends itself to organized action.

Make sense of reality

The charismatic leader can explain complex situations in simple and appealing language, avoiding technical jargon and bureaucratic labels. This unassuming rhetoric brings the leader psychologically close to his or her followers and serves as a personal reference. However, truly charismatic leaders still maintain a certain distance from their followers in order to be idealized as a symbol.

Visualize a positive future

During times of change, things get worse before they get better. Thus, charismatic leaders know how to manage expectations and transform present challenges into future opportunities that will not only benefit the group but individuals. They draw a road map with a light at the end of the tunnel.

So, in leadership looks aren't everything, but charisma – to some extent – is a vital ingredient if people are to follow you.

Resources

Margarita Mayo is doing some interesting work through in-depth interviews with a range of leaders. See more at www.margaritamayo.com.

Leaders are self-aware #38

In the not-so-distant past, business was conducted in an emotion-free environment. Executives were as likely to display emotion as they were to tap dance on the roof of the CEO's car. Now, the emotional nature of leadership – and of day-to-day working life – is routinely acknowledged.

Psychologist and former New York Times journalist Daniel Goleman has advocated the need for leaders to be emotionally intelligent (EI). IQ alone is not enough. Managers need to understand and manage their own emotions and relationships to be effective leaders. Goleman's ideas on emotional intelligence build on the work of David McClelland, an American psychologist who helped establish competencies modeling and was Goleman's mentor at Harvard, and Howard Gardner, the developmental psychologist and professor of cognition and education at the Harvard Graduate School of Education at Harvard University, who developed the theory of Multiple Intelligences.

In *Primal Leadership* Goleman advocates cultivating emotionally intelligent leaders. Goleman and co-authors Richard E. Boyatzis and Annie McKee explain the four domains of emotional intelligence – self-awareness, self-management, social awareness and relationship management – and how they give rise to different styles of leadership. It is a leadership repertoire leaders can master and use to great effect.

Self-knowledge is a recurrent theme talking to leaders. 'Know yourself, be yourself, look after yourself' is central. 'You can't be yourself unless you know yourself, and you can't sustain it, unless you look after yourself,' advises Dame Mary Marsh.

135

Echoing these sentiments is the Tuck Business School's Syd Finkel-
stein. 'I talk about self-awareness,' he says. 'Working in a consulting
capacity with a CEO or senior executive, the extent to which they're
self-aware is really remarkable; it comes out in a conversation so often.
To me it's really one of the most powerful leadership capabilities. That's
how I label it, to make it more practical to people, because self-awareness is a very touchy-feely type of idea once you get right down to it. But
I call it a leadership capability.

'The more anyone knows about how they think, how they behave,
their own biases, the less likely they are to become slaves to that part of
the brain where they just do what gut instinct tells them to do. That can
get you in a lot of trouble, so self-awareness is a big differentiator, think
again.'

Similarly, the first capability associated with the authentic leadership that Bill George identifies is self-awareness. As George notes, many
leaders are so focused on career development that they neglect the challenging, sometimes painful, introspective exercise required to discover
their authentic selves. They also equate success with external measures
of success – such as share price, status, titles, money and fame – without considering whether those measures are truly meaningful for them.
Through an honest examination of their lives, leaders become more vul-
nerable and humane, less unapproachable and remote.

True North: Discover Your Authentic Leadership (2007) by Bill George
with Peter Sims drew on interviews with 125 leaders, aged 23 to 93,
selected mainly due to their reputations for authenticity and effectiveness as leaders. At the time it constituted the largest in-depth study of
leadership development. The idea was to learn how these people developed their leadership abilities. Early on, however, the authors note the
following: 'Analyzing 3,000 pages of transcripts, our team was startled
to see that these people did not identify any universal characteristics,
traits, skills, or styles that led to their success'.

Instead, asserts George, their leadership abilities emerged from their
life stories. 'Consciously and subconsciously, they were constantly testing themselves through real-world experiences and reframing their life

stories to understand who they were at their core. In doing so, they discovered the purpose of their leadership and learned that being authentic made them more effective,' he says.

To begin the journey to authentic leadership, leaders must understand the story of their own life. This provides the narrative and context for authentic leadership, drawing on real-life events to inform leadership today and in the future.

Self-awareness is an integral part of authentic leadership. But it does not require years of psychoanalysis, say Rob Goffee and Gareth Jones. It is about making a connection, knowing what and how much of yourself, your strengths and weakness and idiosyncrasies to reveal to others. The authentic leader cannot connect unless they know their followers well, their hopes, fears, interests and emotional state. For this leaders must get close. At the same time they may need to challenge or cajole, even reprimand, the same followers, and so it is useful to know how to create distance in these cases. Finally, to convey their vision and still appear authentic, leaders must choose the medium and moment that suits their personality and leadership style. And the message must be clear and easy for everyone to understand.

Interestingly, Goffee and Jones also detailed a number of popular conceptions about leadership which they believed were myths. One of those myths, contrary to what many leadership experts argue, is that everyone can be a leader. Not so, say Goffee and Jones. 'Many executives don't have the self-knowledge or the authenticity necessary for leadership,' they say. And also many executives don't want to be leaders anyway. But, for those that do, self-knowledge is key.

Resources

Bill George, Peter Sims, Andrew N. McLean and Diana Mayer, 'Discovering Your Authentic Leadership,' *Harvard Business Review*, February 2007.

Time to declare   #39

In May 1927, when the fifteen-millionth Model T was produced, Henry Ford closed the production line. The Model T was dead, but the trouble was that no one knew what was coming next. Silence reigned. Tension mounted. Finally, in November, Ford announced the arrival of the Model A which was first sold at the beginning of December 1927. Within six weeks there were 750,000 orders. As acts of marketing bravado go, Ford's dramatic closure of the Model T line and the interregnum before the launch of the new model is difficult to match.

Calling time and moving on is a difficult judgment call. Few are able to match Henry's Ford's bravery when it comes to their tenure as a leader. Human nature dictates that great boxers don't retire at the right time, they keep fighting. Politicians fight one election too many, CEOs take on an acquisition too many, and so on.

For leaders, all leaders, there is a finite scale to their effectiveness. Jimmy Maymann, CEO of the *Huffington Post*, reviewed his career with us and noted: 'Most of the things I've done have been in five-year intervals. It makes a lot of sense, because when you've done things for five years it starts to be repetitive, you're starting to do too much of the same, you've done the improvement, you've done the optimizations. Unless you innovate, then it's really difficult, for me at least, to keep doing the same thing.'

We met up with the charismatic Indian CEO Vineet Nayar as he was contemplating his own departure from HCL Technologies. At HCL, Nayar had overseen growth and the creation of a unique corporate culture. HCL's philosophy is distilled down to two words – Employees First: 'A unique management approach that unshackles the creative energies of our 85,335 plus employees, and puts this collective force to work in the service of customers' business problems'.

When we spoke to Nayar, HCL's revenues had reached $4.1 billion, up more than 17 percent in the previous year. 'Six hundred percent growth in seven years, what else can you ask for?' observed Nayar with a smile.

Vineet Nayar joined HCL in 1985 as a management trainee and worked his way up through the company, becoming president of HCL Technologies (there is also a sister company, HCL Infosystems) in 2005.

When we spoke, another member of the legendary Indian batting line-up had just announced his retirement. When would the great Sachin Tendulkar, the little master, announce the end of his glittering career? The Indian media was full of little else. 'A huge debate is going on,' said Nayar:

What is the right time to call it quits? And uniformly everybody said, at the peak – but how do you know that the peak has come? In the stock exchange people make a business of trying to exit quickly at the top of the market. Do they get it right? No, they don't get it right despite the billions of dollars involved. So is the expectation that you will exit at the peak the wrong expectation? And my belief is that it is the wrong expectation.

Nayar pointed out that stock market traders have a stop-loss order to stop losses at a certain point. He suggested that a similar tool should be put in place among managers so that they do not overstay their usefulness.

And so the conversation turned to Nayar's own role at HCL. 'I truly believe that the CEO becomes obsolete in five years. He comes with a lot of gusto in the beginning, and brings about a significant change. And then he has to see it through.'

Nayar argued that the CEO needs to reinvent the job, and points to Bill Gates as a good – if rare – example of someone doing just that. We recall another CEO (Mike Critelli of Pitney Bowes) telling us that

CEOs could only be really effective for seven years. Nayar's calculation is that every five years the CEO should be spending 90 percent of their time on something different. His own emphasis is increasingly on three themes: being socially responsible; Employees First 2.0; and incubating new ideas and businesses.

To some extent, the leader's job can be recast as to actually make leadership invisible, perhaps even redundant. Lao Tzu quipped 'The best leader is one whose existence is barely known by the people.' This is a line often quoted by Zhang Ruimin, the inspirational CEO of the Chinese appliance maker Haier. At Haier, the role of managers has been imaginatively reconfigured and the company recreated as an open marketplace for ideas and talent. The traditional pyramid structure has been all but flattened.

Crucially, this reinvents the role of managers. Haier regards them as entrepreneurs and 'makers'. 'It's better to let employees deal with the market rather than rack our brains to deal with and control them,' Zhang Ruimin has observed. Managers are effectively cut loose. Haier talks of its 'Win-win Model of Individual-Goal Combination' which means that the objectives of individual employees and the organization are on the same trajectory.

Haier also talks of moving from 'complete obedience to leaders' to 'complete obedience to users'. Haier's oft-stated belief is that users are more important than managers. 'The bosses are not customers, why should the workers listen to them?' asks Zhang Ruimin. Haier aspires to management without bosses. One of Haier's core values is that 'users are always right while we need to constantly improve ourselves' and its professed future priority is to produce products to meet the personalized demands of consumers.

The results of this are already many and varied. In white goods it is no longer true that the only color is white. Haier makes mass customization work. Order a Haier product on the internet and you can specify the color and features. This is then relayed to the factory so that even washing machines are now customized. What Henry Ford would have made of this we can only guess.

Resources

The story of the emergence of Haier is told by Bill Fischer, Umberto Lago, and Fang Liu in *Reinventing Giants: How Chinese global competitor Haier has changed the way big companies transform* (Jossey Bass, 2013).

The authors

Des Dearlove and Stuart Crainer are the creators of the Thinkers50 (www.thinkers50.com), the original global ranking of business thought leaders which scans, ranks and shares the best business ideas. Their work in this area led *Management Today* to describe them as 'market makers par excellence'.

They are adjunct professors at IE Business School in Madrid and are former columnists for *The Times*, contributing editors to *Strategy+Business*, and editors of the bestselling *Financial Times Handbook of Management*. Their books, available in more than twenty languages, include *The Management Century*, *Gravy Training* and *Generation Entrepreneur*.

Stuart was editor of the award-winning magazine, *Business Strategy Review*. Des is an associate fellow of Saïd Business School at Oxford University and, under the name D. D. Everest, a bestselling author of children's books.

Index

Printed by Printforce, United Kingdom